Clever Girl Finance

Clever Girl Finance

The Side Hustle Guide

*Build a Successful Side Hustle &
Increase Your Income*

Bola Sokunbi

WILEY

Published by John Wiley & Sons, Inc., Hoboken, New Jersey.
Published simultaneously in Canada.

For general information on our other products and services or for technical support, please contact our Customer Care Department within the United States at (800) 762-2974, outside the United States at (317) 572-3993, or fax (317) 572-4002.

Wiley publishes in a variety of print and electronic formats and by print-on-demand. Some material included with standard print versions of this book may not be included in ebooks or in print-on-demand. If this book refers to media such as a CD or DVD that is not included in the version you purchased, you may download this material at http://booksupport.wiley.com. For more information about Wiley products, visit www.wiley.com.

Library of Congress Cataloging-in-Publication Data is Available:

ISBN 9781119771371 (Paperback)
ISBN 9781119771395 (ePDF)
ISBN 9781119771388 (ePub)

Cover Design: Wiley
Cover Image: © Clever Girl Finance Inc.

SKY10027748_062121

This book is dedicated to my mom, Emily, for being an incredible role model while I was growing up watching her be the ultimate side-hustle queen, and to all the clever girls working hard to create multiple streams of income to achieve their financial goals.

Contents

About the Author

Bola Sokunbi is a Certified Financial Education Instructor (CFEI), investor, finance expert, speaker, podcaster, influencer, and the founder and CEO of Clever Girl Finance, a personal finance platform created to empower women to achieve real wealth and live life on their own terms.

She started Clever Girl Finance in 2015 to provide women with the tools and resources she wished she had when she began her financial journey.

She is also the author of the bestselling books *Clever Girl Finance: Ditch Debt, Save Money and Build Real Wealth* and *Clever Girl Finance: Learn How Investing Works, Grow Your Money*.

Today, she lives with her husband and twins in New Jersey.

Acknowledgments

If you'd told me I'd write three books in three years, I would never have believed you. Yet here I am on my third book, three years later. I am so honored and grateful to have yet another opportunity to share my story, knowledge, and the stories of others as part of my mission to help women achieve financial wellness.

To my husband, my children, and my family, thank you so much for your continued love and support and for constantly cheering me on.

To my incredible mentors, advisors, and friends who constantly encouraged me while I was working on this book, I appreciate you so much!

To the amazing women who have allowed me to share their honest and open entrepreneurial journeys throughout this book: Camilla Banks, Vickii Onabolu, Ayesha Chidolue, Tiwa Lawrence, Kalyn Johnson Chandler, Wonuola Okoye, Sahirenys Pierce, Nike Olagbegi, Fisola Adepetu, Emilie Aries, and Ebony Ruffin; thank you!

A massive thank-you to the Clever Girl Finance team, Esther Bangura, Yazmir Torres, Jui Khopkar, Anita Wikina, and Stacy Jeffries, who kept things running smoothly while I was chin-deep writing this book. And to Kate Braun, my amazing editor, for working through my book edits.

Finally, a big thank-you to the incredibly hard working team at Wiley who have supported me through editing, publishing, and promoting what you now hold in your hands—my third book!

Love always,
Bola

It's Time to Make Your Side-Hustle Dreams a Reality!

I'm so excited that you have this book in your hands and are about to embark on this incredible journey of starting or growing your side hustle. Rest assured, it's not by accident that you are here!

It could be that you are familiar with the Clever Girl Finance platform, or you've read one (or both) of my first two books: *Clever Girl Finance: Ditch Debt, Save Money and Build Real Wealth* or *Learn How Investing Works, Grow Your Money*. Maybe you've taken one (or a few) of the free Clever Girl Finance online courses. Or perhaps a friend or even an online algorithm recommended this book to you.

However you got here, you are here now, reading this book—most likely because pursuing your passions and increasing your income through a side hustle is something you've wanted to do for a while.

You see countless people doing exactly this every single day. You see them promoting their businesses and sharing behind-the-scenes photos on social media, you've admired their products and/or services, you've listened to their interviews on your favorite podcasts, you've watched videos of them online, and somewhere in the back of your mind, you've yearned to do your own thing. . .just like them.

You've imagined what it would be like for you to be on the other side, running your own side hustle. And not just any kind of random side hustle: an incredibly successful one that in turn gives you the opportunity to build your dream business, increase your income, and ultimately afford the life you desire and on your own terms.

But perhaps you've hesitated. After all, you've heard that starting, running, and growing a business is incredibly hard. It could be that you've even tried in the past, but things didn't quite turn out how you'd imagined. Maybe you feel like there's so much you don't know and are overwhelmed by the thought of trying to figure it all out on your own and making too many mistakes along the way. Or it could simply be that you are afraid to go at this alone.

Well, not to worry. I've written this book specifically for women like you, to guide, encourage, and motivate you on this journey to building an amazing business. Like I said, you are not here by accident. In this book, I'll show you just what it takes to build, run, and grow an incredibly successful side hustle—because you have what it takes.

I'll be sharing the key insights from my experiences as a multi-side-hustle business owner and now a full-time entrepreneur. I'll let you in on the mistakes I made along the way and the many lessons I learned that have led me to where I am today: the founder and CEO of one of the largest personal finance platforms for women, a business I started as a simple side hustle.

I'll be challenging you to ditch any fears holding you back from following your passion, showing you exactly how to lay out the right plans (and financials) that work best for you, and guiding you step-by-step as you build a business your customers and clients will rave about and one that you'll love running as well.

As with my previous books, I'll be bringing some of my amazing entrepreneur friends along on this journey with us to also share their unique experiences building their own incredibly successful side hustles that span across a wide variety of industries and niches.

At the end of this book, you'll walk away with a renewed mindset, a solid blueprint for your business, and a wealth of insight and motivation not just to start your business, but to take it to the next level.

Because—WHY NOT YOU?

So, buckle up, girlfriend, it's going to be an exciting ride. Let's go!

HOW TO USE THIS BOOK

I've written this book to help you craft the ideal blueprint for building a successful side hustle. As with any good blueprint, the idea is to reference it as necessary while you lay your foundations and build your business. There are several ways in which you'll be able to leverage the content in this book, but here are a few recommendations to help you make the most of it:

- You can read through this book all at once and then circle back to work on the action steps, or you can read it a section at a time and implement what you learn as you go along.
- As you read, take your time. Take notes, highlight, and bookmark the areas you'd like to revisit that stand out to you the most based on the stage you're at with building your business.
- Plan to work through the action steps at the end of each section to help you craft your strategies and fine-tune your blueprint.
- Once you are done reading the book, review your notes, highlights, and bookmarks.
- Keep things organized by creating a Google Sheets or Microsoft Excel workbook where you can create tabs for each of the different spreadsheets suggested through the book, depending on what's relevant to you.
- Keep this book as a reference as you work on your business. There might be areas you are focused on immediately and areas you'll need to come back to later as you make progress.

Ultimately, I want you to gain as much as possible from this book to help you achieve your business and income goals!

CHAPTER 1

Getting Prepared to Win

Fact: You have what it takes to build an incredibly successful business.

CHALLENGING THE FEAR THAT HOLDS YOU BACK

So, before we dive into all things side hustles and business, let's start at the very beginning. Let's start with you and what could potentially be holding you back: your fear. Yup, that tiny little four-letter word is a pretty big deal because it can negatively impact your ability to pursue your goals in a major way. And more specifically to our topic at hand, fear can impact your ability to start and grow a successful side hustle.

When it comes to starting or growing a side hustle, fear is real and worry is its best friend. Did you nod your head? It's probably because you've felt one or more of several different fears that come with this journey. I have personally felt all kinds of fears and had all kinds of worries on my business journey.

For instance, there's the fear of the unknown and not knowing enough: *"I have no idea how any of this works or how I will pull it off."*

There's the fear of failure: *"What if I start this thing and it doesn't work out?"*

There's the fear of risk: *"This is going to take too much time, money, and resources."*

There's the fear that you are incapable (aka imposter syndrome): *"Who am I to think I can do this?"*

There's also the fear of change: *"Just thinking about starting a side hustle and the road ahead makes me nervous!"*

And these are just to name a few. Add in worrying about where you are going to find the time and worrying about what other people will think, and you have the perfect formula to do. . .nothing. Absolutely nothing. And this is where so many incredible business ideas die and get buried.

Fear is a major reason why so many people don't pursue their dreams or they give up too quickly. Defined by the Merriam-Webster dictionary[1] as *"an unpleasant often strong emotion*

---

[1] https://www.merriam-webster.com/dictionary/fear

caused by anticipation or awareness of danger," fear can actually prevent you from pursuing incredible opportunities, because if you don't have a handle on it, it can cloud your judgment.

Keep in mind, though, the goal is not to do away with fear completely. There are many instances where we need it to warn us and keep us alert to problems or dangers. Instead, we need to learn how to address our fear, minimize its hold over us, and use it to our benefit.

Instead of letting fear dictate the actions we take (or don't take), we need to adjust our approach to dealing with it. When it came to building my own business, I've felt every single one of the fears I just mentioned. But this time, I decided I had spent too much of my life allowing my fears to keep me stuck or make me give up. I was done with looking back in regret at what I wish I could have done but didn't. I decided to approach fear differently and instead leverage it to help me succeed.

So how do you leverage fear to your benefit? Here's what has worked for me in the past and continues to work for me to this day.

Start by accepting that fear does not go away on its own, so you have to confront it head-on. Instead of letting it keep you uncertain and stuck, look at your fears as an opportunity to learn and grow. Whenever I feel fear, I challenge myself to identify what exactly I'm afraid of. I then ask myself what worst-case scenario or outcome could arise from the source of my fear. Once I'm clear on this, I determine the best-case scenario and outcome, because thinking about it this way is super-motivating. Then, I lay out specific actions that I can take to help me counter my fear.

It could be working to improve a certain skill to help me overcome a business challenge I'm facing. It could be asking for help or leaning on my support system of business mentors and fellow entrepreneurs (we'll get into how you can establish a support system for yourself later on). It could be dusting off my "why" and reminding myself why I want to succeed. It could be imagining what my success could look like after I achieve a certain goal. Or it could be as simple as stepping away to take a mental break and coming back to things later on with a clear head and rested body.

These are all things that you can do as well to power through your fears. Instead of letting your fears set you back, you can leverage them to propel you forward by being objective about the root cause and creating a plan to take action, no matter how small your first step may be.

Fear is an indicator that you are outside of your comfort zone—but outside your comfort zone is where the magic happens. This is where you turn your "one-day" dreams and goals into a successful reality. As you make progress with your side hustle or business, you'll face fears about different things and in different ways, but the key is to remain objective and take action to counter your fears.

You'll come away each time feeling more confident in yourself and clearer about what you need to do to succeed in business.

Take Action

Let's challenge your fears! Take some time to do the following action steps to turn your fears into opportunities:

1. **Identify your fears.** Write down every fear that has discouraged you or has been an excuse as to why you have not taken the next step to build your side hustle.

2. **Determine the worst-case scenarios.** For each fear, write down the absolute worst-case scenario of what could happen and what it could look like. You get less sleep, your life gets busier, you cut back on your expenses in certain areas to invest in your business. . .you may find

that it's actually not that bad. Or maybe you're envision-ing a worse, big-picture scenario: no one wants to buy your product, or you invest a lot of money in your busi-ness only for it to fail. (Don't worry: there are ways to counter all your fears, big or small!)

3. **Imagine the best-case scenarios.** Now, lay out what it would look like to succeed in detail. You make your first sale, you have a return customer, you get an amazing press feature, your business becomes profitable, and earns you more income than your full-time job! By focusing on best-case scenarios, you can motivate yourself!

4. **Lay out specific action steps you can take to coun-ter your fears.** Next, write down specific action steps you can take (no matter how small) and timelines to complete them that will help you counter your fears. For instance, if you're worried about life getting too busy and frantic, create a schedule with designated times to take a break. If you're worried about money, start by investing small amounts in your business until you've proven it can make a profit, while saving money from your day job. If you fear that your idea will flop, spend time researching your target market to validate that there's a need for it. Set suc-cess-oriented goals like implementing what you learn in this book, identifying a business mentor, etc.

GET PREPARED TO BUILD A SUCCESSFUL BUSINESS

Now that you have a plan to tackle your fears, it's time to get your head in the game and prepare yourself to build not just any side hustle, but a *successful* side hustle. And it starts by establish-ing the right mindset.

From setting financial goals, to budgeting, to paying off debt, to saving and investing, to, you guessed it, actually starting the side hustle, having the right mindset is foundational and critical to your success at each stage.

Having the right mindset gets you ready for the journey ahead, and nurturing your mindset along the way keeps you motivated and focused. This in turn increases your chances of success. But why is mindset so important when you are starting or growing a side hustle? After all, isn't a *side* hustle something you just do on the side?

Well, it depends on how you choose to view your side hustle. Yes, by definition a side hustle is something you do on the side, before or after your primary job. It's a side activity in your spare time that can bring in some extra income (the money potential is what distinguishes it from a hobby). Simple, right? However, depending on what you do and how you do it, your side hustle can open the doors to so much more.

Let me elaborate further: a side hustle can be game-changing for your life and your ability to achieve your goals, especially in today's world, thanks to the accessibility of the internet. Don't let the traditional idea of a side hustle make you think otherwise. Side hustles today aren't just about the random garage sale every other month. They can be real, impactful, and high-income-generating businesses.

Specifically, in this book, I'm going to be using "side hustle" and "business" somewhat interchangeably. While you could call driving for Uber or doing deliveries for Amazon a side hustle or side gig, those are still ultimately jobs you're doing for someone else. I want to talk about businesses you're creating for yourself, with your own ideas, and on your own terms.

A side hustle gives you the opportunity to increase your income and create multiple streams of income. Having multiple income sources is especially important as a woman, and even more so for women of color. You've heard about the impact of the gender wage gap, where women earn 20 percent less on average than their white male counterparts. However, for women of color, the wage gap is even more extreme. Black women earn 62 cents for every dollar earned by their white male counterparts, Latina women earn 54 cents, and Native American women earn 57 cents.[2] This gender wage gap in turn impacts our ability to save and invest money for our future selves and to support our families.

Asking for what you are worth, negotiating, and actively calling out inequalities—especially as it relates to pay due to gender and race—are ways you can take action to counter this on an institutional level. But while we work toward long-term change, having a side hustle can position you to get ahead of this in a major way. Your side hustle can accelerate your journey to becoming debt-free, meeting your savings and investing goals, supporting your family, and building generational wealth.

As I write this book amid a global pandemic, with so much economic uncertainty and millions of people out of jobs or worried about job security, a side hustle can become the backup you need to weather the storms of financial uncertainties. This is applicable for any difficult season, whether it's a global pandemic, a national recession, or a personal financial setback. Your side hustle can be the backup to get you through by providing an additional stream of income to help pay your bills or build a well-stocked emergency fund.

There are also many instances of well-executed side hustles that generate enough revenue to replace the income from the owner's full-time job, giving them the option to be *their own* boss on *their own* schedule if they decide to do so. Essentially, your side hustle can create a multitude of options for your life, and those options equal freedom and the ability to follow your passions! How about that for something you just do "on the side"?

But back to mindset—the way you decide to think about your side hustle can make all the difference. If you tell yourself that all it can ever be is a side thing that will earn a few dollars here and there, then that's what it will be and you can stop reading this book here.

---

[2]https://www.nationalpartnership.org/our-work/resources/economic-justice/fair-pay/quantifying-americas-gender-wage-gap.pdf

However, if deep down you believe your side hustle has the potential for incredible success and you are not willing to put a limit on how far it can go, then you are setting the stage for endless potential and incredible success (even if you don't know how you'll get there just yet).

Like I said, your mindset will keep you motivated and focused, and this is important because starting any kind of business is hard. Even "just" a side hustle. It takes hard work, time spent away from doing things with your loved ones, early mornings and late nights, learning new things, and testing, testing, and testing again.

There's also the emotional and mental toll it can take. Starting something new or doing things differently, especially in business, can be isolating, and it can be really hard to want to keep going when things seem to be happening extremely slowly or not at all. Your friends might not understand this new ambition and you might not immediately find your new business support system or mentorship. It's easy to get overwhelmed when you think about the journey ahead of you and the things you need to do despite only having 24 hours in a day, and even more intimidating to think about doing everything on your own.

All of that being said, preparation for success is vital to get you ready to face these challenges. This means preparing your mindset, figuring out your schedule, adjusting your lifestyle (if only for a season), and establishing a way to stay accountable as you work on your side hustle.

Preparing Your Mindset

Your mindset is like a muscle you have to keep in shape. And as you undertake the journey to building a successful business, this muscle is more important than ever. To prepare your mindset, you need to first decide that you are going to commit to the journey. Don't just go halfway; give it your all. Part of motivating this commitment means getting clear on the reason you want to succeed—what is your *why?* Who or what are you doing this for? Why do you want it so badly? Write down your reason (or reasons) and put it in a place where you'll see it every day. It could be a sticky-note on your bathroom mirror, an image on your phone's lock screen, or even your computer background. Having your *why* in place will help you work through distractions and will empower you to keep going.

Next, commit to affirming yourself. Create daily positive reminders of why you are amazing and why you are capable of doing this, regardless of your current position. This will help you counter the negative talk in your mind (that little annoying voice that always pops up at the most inconvenient times to discourage you). Leverage your affirmations to shut that rude voice down—like, hey, voice, yes, *you*, BE QUIET. Your affirmations could be quotes, prayers, or sentences you create yourself. Whichever way you choose to craft them, they should be positive, in present tense, and empowering.

Adjusting Your Schedule

By adjusting your schedule to accommodate working on your business, you are being intentional about putting your desire for success into action. It's you designating a set period of your days, weeks, and months to put in the effort and making time for your success.

You can adjust your schedule so you wake up early to work on your business before you go to your main job, or you may decide to stay up late after your house has quieted down. You can dedicate time to your side hustle on the weekend. Whatever schedule you settle on, set reminders (e.g., phone alarms or computer notifications), and create a prioritized daily to-do list. Intentional actions like this will enable you to build consistency around the actions you need to take to build your side hustle.

Tip: Make your calendar updates and reminders fun! This will motivate you each time you look at your schedule and get those reminder alerts. Just seeing your calendar show, "Work on my amazing business!" from 5 a.m. to 7 a.m., or getting a reminder like, "Hey, Queen! It's time for XYZ task; you got this!" can be just what you need in that moment to make things happen. You could even cue Rhianna's "Work" song (♪ *work, work, work, work, work* ♪) as your "It's time to work" alarm. Who said this journey couldn't be fun?

Staying Accountable

Another really important step as you prepare to build your successful side hustle is getting and staying accountable. The early stage of your business is like planting fresh seeds. In order for your seeds to grow, you need to water them, make sure they get enough sunlight, and keep weeds away from choking out your budding plants.

This is where your accountability partners come in. These people are your water, your sunlight, and your weed-killers. These are the people who will pick you up when you are feeling down, will give you objective feedback, and will tell you to cut it out when you try to start the pity party. They could be people in your life who cheer you on or like minded friends also working on their side-hustle journeys.

If you don't have them physically around you, leverage the internet to build a supportive community. Find those side-hustle owners and entrepreneurs you admire and make them your best friends in your head. Follow their journeys, read their posts, listen to their interviews, watch their videos. Keep yourself accountable by keeping up with them to stay motivated and focused.

Be sure to schedule time frequently to check in with your real-life accountability partners or your online besties.

Take Action

Carve out some time to prepare yourself for the journey ahead.

1. **Determine your *why*.** Know why you are doing this and why you want to succeed. Write it down and put it somewhere you can see it every day.

2. **Create affirmations that will empower you to succeed.** Leverage quotes, prayers, or statements you create yourself. They should be positive and in present tense. Set a reminder to review them often.

3. **Lay out your schedule.** Make time to work on your business and take action each day, no matter how small. Set your alerts and reminders, and don't forget to make them fun and empowering.

4. **Identify your accountability partner or partners.** Who can positively support you on this journey and cheer you on? Let them know what you are doing and ask to check in with them frequently. Depending on schedules, it could be weekly, bi-weekly, or monthly, but you want to build some consistency around it, especially when you are first getting started. If you don't have accountability partners in person, start researching to find people online who can motivate you. Follow them on social media and subscribe to their newsletters, video channels, podcasts, etc.

MY SIDE HUSTLE BUSINESS STORY

I started side-hustling as a preteen selling candy to my friends over summer break, then moved on to selling Avon beauty products while I was in college. A few years after graduation, I started an online retail business and also a wedding and lifestyle photography business. I even started Clever Girl Finance as a side hustle. And despite running Clever Girl Finance full-time now, my mind is constantly buzzing with side-hustle ideas that I share with friends and family all the time.

Why am I so passionate about side hustles? They've been incredible learning experiences and have allowed me to earn a lot of money over time. My side hustle inspiration comes from my mother. Her side hustles made a big impact on what she was able to accomplish financially when I was growing up, and I got to watch it happen.

My mother has always had a side hustle for as long as I can remember. She's pretty much the queen of side hustles. From when she was a stay-at-home mom raising her four kids, to when she went to get her college degree (with me in tow at all her classes), to after she had multiple degrees and was working full-time in banking, she was always running one side business or another.

On evenings after her full-time job and on the weekends while I was growing up, she would take me to visit the different businesses she had over the years. Some of these businesses included a bakery, a Coca-Cola franchise, a hair salon, and a girl's school. She was also always buying and selling all kinds of goods for profit. In retrospect, I realize my mother was able to run these businesses as side hustles by creating systems and processes and hiring the right people. And even today, she still has a side hustle and is always churning ideas in her mind of what to do next.

Having these side hustles not only allowed my mother to contribute to our household finances in a major way; they also allowed her to achieve financial wellness and ultimately become the breadwinner of our family when my father went through a financial downturn. Her hustles also allowed her to support me (alongside a partial scholarship) through college as an international student, an opportunity I will never forget.

She worked incredibly hard to build and grow her side hustles, but at the end of the day, all of her efforts were worth it. On the visits we made together to the various businesses she was running, she would always remind me how making my own money could give me options and freedom. Seeing her drive and dedication to her side hustles while I was a child set the perfect example.

Going back to my first side hustle selling candy, I remember saving up my pocket money to buy a bunch of hard-to-find candy flavors (specifically, some lollipops called Chupa Chups) and then selling them at a profit to my friends in my neighborhood. It was exciting to see my investment grow quickly, and while my profits were tiny, just knowing I could sell something and earn money gave me a big rush. It didn't last long, though, because after I shared my success with a friend, she convinced me to lend her all of the money I made—and I never saw it or her again (#Igotpunked—story for another book!). I did, however, gain some valuable lessons from that first business. Without realizing it at the time, I was learning about pricing my products, making sure I was getting paid, and (very importantly) how not to lose my profits.

Fast forward to my last year of college, I started another side hustle selling Avon for a few months before graduation. Yup, I was an Avon lady! My mum would order me the catalogs and I would basically take orders from anyone and everyone possible, making note of everything in my little Avon receipt book. It was with this business that I realized the financial gain that could come from having a side hustle. Back then, if you sold over a certain amount of Avon products within the time frame before a catalog expired, you could earn up to 40 percent or more in commissions. And for me, the ability to earn money was my motivation. I would sell as much as I could to meet this threshold, and I ended up earning a pretty decent income from my Avon hustle. From my earnings, I was able to co-host my sister-in-law's bridal shower, buy my bridesmaid dress, buy return plane tickets to fly to and from the wedding, and give my brother and his wife a lovely wedding gift. As a college student, being able to do this was huge for me.

Several years later, I would start an online bridal accessory and clothing retail store and a wedding and lifestyle photography business. I ran both of these as side hustles part-time while working full-time as a technology consultant in corporate America.

My online retail shop was called the White Dress Shop. It was inspired by my photography business, as brides would be constantly asking me if I knew where other brides I'd photographed had gotten their wedding accessories and pre- and post-wedding event outfits. Based on this, I decided to set up a business to fill that void. I figured out how to become a wholesaler for various brands, how to use line sheets to plan future inventory, how to set up an ecommerce website, how to organize my physical inventory, how to set up processes for packing, shipping, and returns (aka fulfillment), and very importantly, how to become a pro at customer service! Since I was already in the wedding industry as a photographer (which I'll get into shortly), it wasn't that difficult for me to figure how best to market my side hustle, and it became profitable after a few months.

However, while the profits were nice, I shut down the business just shy of its second anniversary. I quickly started running out of space to store my inventory at home, I had begun planning my own wedding, and my husband and I would be moving cities twice over a short period of time due to our jobs. Given that I was running this side hustle alongside my photography business and a full-time job, I decided to minimize my overall stress and focus on the one side hustle that was earning me the most money.

My wedding photography business, called Onada Photography, was my longest-running side hustle, and I did it for seven years. Over that period of time, it also earned me the most amount of money of all my side hustles—up to the tune of almost $70,000 in one particular year. Funny enough, I stumbled into wedding photography mostly by accident. My dad was always taking photos, so I have tons and tons of photographs that document my childhood. Despite being exposed to it early on, I never imagined myself as a professional photographer until one day an opportunity presented itself and ignited the idea.

I was visiting Jamaica for a friend's wedding, and I had just purchased a new low-cost entry-level professional camera from Nikon, which I took along for the trip. For whatever reason, my friend's wedding photographer was running late on the day of her wedding. She had seen my camera earlier on and asked me to take a few photos before her photographer arrived, which I did. I loved the photos, and more importantly, so did she. This got me thinking that perhaps there was an opportunity to make some money with my photography!

I advertised (on Craigslist back then) to get my first few wedding photography gigs, and shot them for free. Yup, free! I did this because I didn't have any experience photographing a wedding outside of the pre-wedding shots for my friend, and I felt that if people accepted my services for free, it would minimize the risk if for whatever reason the photos didn't come out as expected. I had so much to learn, and I also needed to build a portfolio of images to showcase on my photography website, so this approach made sense for me—and it worked. Because I didn't set any expectations and I put in my best effort, my clients loved their photographs. I bought books, watched videos, practiced on my family and friends, paid for workshops, and essentially became a self-taught photographer. Once I built a solid portfolio, I was able to confidently charge for my work and invest in better equipment.

It definitely wasn't a walk in the park, though. On the weekends, I was busy photographing weddings and other events. I remember incredibly crazy summers doing back-to-back weddings on Friday evening, Saturday, and then on Sunday. On weekdays, after working at my day job (where I put in 60 hours a week on average), I went straight home and got on my computer to sort and edit photos late into the night. Many times, I'd also wake up to do the same thing early in the morning before I went to work—rinse and repeat.

I was exhausted, but I was happy to be making all that extra money on the side. I charged $3,000 to $5,000 a wedding and $300 to $450 for my lifestyle photography sessions (e.g., baby sessions, engagement sessions, family sessions, etc.). The year I made almost $70,000 with this side hustle, I photographed

19 weddings and several lifestyle sessions. I transitioned out of this business after having my twins, but I had another side hustle idea brewing: Clever Girl Finance.

Yup, Clever Girl Finance started as a simple side hustle that I created to share my financial journey and what I had learned with other women. I was always being asked questions about things like budgeting and investing, and I enjoyed talking about money with my family, girlfriends, co-workers, and acquaintances. At times, the conversations could be uncomfortable and uneasy—because for many, money is still very much a taboo topic. I wanted to use my side hustle as a way to change that.

As I slowly transitioned out of my photography business, I would spend late nights and weekends creating content, doing one-on-one coaching sessions, and slowly but surely building an audience. As a result of the time and effort spent on building this business and applying what I learned from my side hustles over the years, Clever Girl Finance is now my full-time job, we have an incredible team, it has grown to become one of the largest personal finance platforms for women in America, and, you are here, reading this book!

Having multiple side hustles has contributed to my life immensely, both personally, from a growth and experience perspective, and financially, allowing me to achieve many of the financial goals I've set for myself over the years. All the hard work has been completely worth it. I went from the girl selling lollipops to her friends to the woman who built a successful business that provides jobs and positively impacts the lives of women everywhere.

The best part of you reading the highlights of my entrepreneurial journey is that you, too, can be successful and leverage your side hustle to have an incredibly positive impact on your life. Your goals, aspirations, and ideas might be completely different from mine, but as long as you are committed to the process, intentional about your time, and ready to put in the work, you can achieve whatever goals you've laid out for yourself.

Yes, starting and growing a side hustle takes time and effort, and you'll be doing some hard work to get your business off its feet. But through all those challenges, you'll have the upper hand, because I'll be here to guide you with key tips, insights, and lessons learned from my own experiences. If you stick with me, you'll build a solid runway to help you take off smoothly on your journey to building the business of your dreams.

As mentioned earlier, throughout this book you'll be reading about and learning from the stories of some amazing women from all walks of life and with all kinds of incredible businesses. Despite their varying backgrounds, they have all achieved success in business, and their stories will keep you inspired and motivated as you read this book.

So, let's keep going; we've got work to do!

Take Action

Challenge yourself to dream!

1. **Think big.** Write down what you imagine your side hustle could become. You don't need to have all the answers of how you'll get there or have all the money to make it happen right now; you just need to know that you *can* get there.

2. **Spend time reviewing your dreams.** Spend some time to really take in what you've written down. If any new fear crops up, go back to the list of fears you created earlier, add it on, and then brainstorm the potential actions you can take to counter that fear.

If you currently own or have attempted a side hustle in the past, now is a great time to reflect on your experience and answer the following questions to help you as you work toward creating fresh success in your business:

1. What went well and what didn't?

2. What are the key lessons you learned from the business experiences you had?

3. How can you apply them going forward to avoid the mistakes and/or amplify your success in business?

WHAT NOT TO EXPECT FROM YOUR SIDE HUSTLE

Before we dive further into this book, I want to make sure you are really clear about the realities of what side hustles are and aren't, so you set the right expectations as you go on this journey. It's easy to get caught up in the glitz and glam showcased on social media that can make building a business seem completely effortless. You might see ads and photos of people working from beaches and think that all you have to do is put up a website and a nice logo and you'll be instantly profitable. However, that is rarely the case, and for the vast majority of side business owners, it couldn't be further from the truth.

There are tons of successful entrepreneurs, and it's easy to look at their success lightly without considering all the time, effort, sweat, and even tears that were put into making their success seem effortless—especially if they only show a limited view of how it all really happens behind the scenes.

There are also many who are simply faking it for the 'gram and distorting the reality of having a successful business because they haven't actually achieved it themselves. This can, unfortunately, sway your perception of what it really takes. (By the way, you won't need to fake anything, because you'll be making it happen!)

So, let's talk about some things you want to be really clear on as you embark on this journey.

Juggling Your Side Hustle and Your Full-Time Job

Once you get into the flow of building your business, things can get really exciting. But if you are also employed full-time, you only have a limited amount of time each day between work and your other responsibilities. You may find that as your side hustle efforts start ramping up and consuming more of your time and energy, it can impact your focus and quality of work at your full-time job.

If you find yourself using your side hustle as an excuse for diminishing performance at work, that's a red flag. After all, you likely still rely on your full-time job to cover your bills and sustain your lifestyle while you get your side hustle off the ground. It's important to make sure you are meeting (and even exceeding) expectations to avoid being called out or even let go for performance reasons, which could put you in a bad financial situation.

When you get to the point where your side hustle is pulling in the big bucks, you can decide to work part-time or leave your full-time job altogether. In the meantime, you want to ensure that you're minimizing any negative impacts to your job while you still need it to pay the bills.

This means prioritizing your to-do lists and creating a schedule where you dedicate focused time to work on your side hustle and focused time to meet your work obligations. If you work 9–5, don't borrow time from your work schedule to brainstorm about your side hustle (except on your breaks or other downtime).

Finding more time in the rest of your day could mean spending less time on your favorite hobbies, waking up earlier, and going to bed later than normal, meal-prepping easy foods to cut down time spent on cooking, etc. You'll probably have to make sacrifices, but remembering your "why" will help you stay motivated for the season in which you have to do this.

Fitting Your Side Hustle into Your Financial Plan

People often make the mistake of assuming that having a profitable side hustle business equals financial success and is the solution to all money problems. Now, don't get me wrong, a side hustle can bring incredible financial gain if executed the right way. However, simply having a successful side hustle is not the end-all, be-all or magical solution to your wealth-building strategy.

Wealth building happens when you are being intentional and working with a plan that accounts for all elements of your financial wellness. This means not just earning more money but also budgeting, creating a plan to pay off debt, saving for emergencies and short-term goals, and investing for the long term.

You should be actively considering your financial plan along-side your business. Otherwise, the profits you earn can easily slip away, unaccounted for. The last thing you want is to put in all this effort to build your business, and start earning profits, only to realize you have no clue what's happening to all the money you are making.

Developing the Personal Characteristics You Need for Success

Your journey to a successful side hustle is unique to you and what you ultimately want to accomplish. That said, there are four characteristics that I see over and over in the most success-ful entrepreneurs:

1. **Patience**, because great things need time.
2. **Focus,** because distraction deters from success.
3. **Perseverance**, because you'll need to manage your emotions, make sacrifices, and keep going when it's hard.
4. **The right mindset**, because all those dreams and goals you'll accomplish start first in your head and in your heart.

These characteristics are core to your success, so keep them in mind as you work on your business. Create a plan to nurture them by reviewing your goals, working on your plans, staying motivated and inspired, and learning from the experiences of others.

Take Action

1. **Plan out your personal finances.** If you haven't already, make time to lay out your financial plans while you work on your business. Include plans to budget, pay down debt, save, and invest. (If you need help, check out my first book: *Clever Girl Finance: Ditch Debt, Save Money and Build Real Wealth*.)

2. **Create a priority list.** If you are employed full-time, create an ongoing priority list of your work to-dos, keeping your deliverables and deadlines in mind. This way you can ensure nothing important falls to the side and threatens your employment status. Work on your side hustle around your full-time work schedule.

MEET CAMILLA BANKS

Camilla is a lover of all things home, as the founder of The MUTED Home (themutedhome.com) and HollandLUXE Properties (hollandluxeproperties.com). For over 10 years, she has consistently centered her life on the subject of home. Today, she runs both of her businesses with her husband, making it the perfect partnership. Their goal is to have their businesses work for them so they can pursue their hearts' desires, and to that end, they are leveraging their skills and talents in business to live life on their own terms.

You run two successful businesses that both started as side hustles. Can you share a bit about them and why you started them? How did you make time while working full-time?
My first real business as a custom furniture designer in 2009 started off from my passion for wanting to create unique and exclusive pieces—I wanted to deliver the ideas I had in my head to other people. I worked on building my business during work (guilty!) and also after work, making deliveries in

the evenings and working on marketing late into the night. Managing a business while doing my best to stay focused on my corporate job was very hard. Some days I'd be so sleepy and live off of coffee. Other days I'd be gentle with myself and work on my business for a few hours after work. I kept a pretty tight schedule. On the weekends I would actually rest, no phone calls, no consultations, and I was very strict on that.

Since then, my husband and I have rebranded our custom furniture company, now called The MUTED Home, into a quality beautiful home goods company.

I started my second business in real estate in order to create a secondary income and follow my passion for educating my clients on what it takes to get into their dream homes. Literally, the moment I was ready to sit for the state real estate exam, I was let go from my full-time job. I had never been so at peace being let go from my job because fortunately, I was already set up to make money to sustain myself since I had built my clientele over four years. It was just God's divine timing. I remember my tax lady even threatened that if I came back one more year making the same money that I was making at my job, she'd refuse to do my taxes. Lucky for me, getting fired was the perfect push to make that leap. I remember telling a client that I was finally working as a full-time entrepreneur. She was blown away; she said she never knew I worked a corporate job because I was usually pretty available and attentive. I just always worked around my job.

Collectively, every day my husband and I are always busy running both businesses, but we work on a schedule to be most productive. We get up at a certain time, and we stop at a certain time. This helps to keep our focus on work during the day, and family time in the evenings.

What were the biggest fears you faced when you first got into business and how did those fears impact the progress you made initially?

One of the biggest fears I had, as I think with most people, was failing. I thought people would ask for all these qualifications (that I didn't need) and I considered going back to school, which I'm glad I didn't. I would spend as much time as possible trying to make everything perfect, but it was really procrastination out of fear. And then, of course, there were my money fears. I wasn't confident that the money I was spending on the business would be worth it. Another fear I had at the time with my first business was that the industry was very male-dominated and oftentimes, I received crazy looks or people just didn't want to work with me because I was a woman.

What did you do to tackle your fears as a new business owner, and how do you deal with fear now?

To tackle my fears, I actually just started "doing." My favorite saying is "Done is better than perfect." This is so true, as sometimes we need to just kick fear in the butt and keep moving, and that remains my mantra today. The things you think people are thinking of you, they most likely are not, and if they are, you should do what you need to anyway. You will never live a life where you are not being judged. Some days when I became discouraged, or when I had negative thoughts on whether or not I could do this, my husband was by my side. He was there to comfort me and encourage me to keep going, this is truly my calling, and things would soon work in my favor.

What are you most proud of, looking back at the progress you've made?

I'm proud of the education I received from working my full-time job in hospitality, as a hotel manager overseeing the day-to-day operations of the staff and guests. Although I wanted to quit, having that job taught me discipline, conflict resolution, and the key skills to ultimately operate my own business.

I'm also seriously so proud I had the nerve to take the heat of being talked about and navigate not getting the support I thought I'd have from friends and family (don't get hurt over this). Every day, I'm still surprised at how far I've come, and I'm so very proud of the decisions and the sacrifices I've made. Now that my grandparents are older, I'm thankful I can fly home to Detroit for longer periods of time to help them. I've always wanted to be able to work from anywhere and to also have a business that can essentially run off delegation. Being able to teach others real estate, assist my clients with buying their homes, and watch the growing success of our new company, we feel so blessed to have this opportunity.

What advice would you give any woman who's thinking about starting her side hustle or is working on growing her side hustle but is worried about the fear of failure?
The main piece of advice I would give to other women is to study your craft and be the best at it. Do it in your own way, with your own spin and your own style. Most people will do business with you because they like you and because you are great at what you do, and not necessarily because of the product or service you are providing. Finally, be fearless in all of your pursuits, be clever, remain encouraged and motivated, and never allow anything to hold you back from your dreams. Just do it!

CHAPTER 2

Laying Out Your Business Idea

Make your ideas happen.

WHAT'S IT GONNA BE? BRAINSTORMING YOUR BUSINESS IDEAS

One of the most common comments I hear from aspiring business owners is, *"I want to start a side hustle but I'm not sure what to start,"* or, *"I want to grow my business but I'm all out of ideas."* Well, every great business starts and grows with ideas, so now we are going to talk about brainstorming your business ideas to help inspire you on your journey. Perhaps you haven't quite figured out what type of side hustle you want to start, or you are trying to come up with new ideas to grow your existing business. Either way, you'll need to learn how to brainstorm effectively.

You've probably had a ton of different business ideas pass through your mind over the years. If you've ever seen a product or service and thought to yourself, *"I had that idea first!"* well, so have I! There are so many things I see every now and then that I know I definitely thought about as an idea, even if it was for a fleeting moment. (Excuse me while I shed a tear for all the times I could have been a billionaire if only I had pursued the idea. . .*sigh.*)

As human beings, what typically happens when an idea comes to mind is:

1. We embrace it and decide to pursue it.
2. We decide we aren't passionate enough about it to pursue it.
3. We almost immediately come up with excuses as to why we can't do it and quickly dismiss it before we even give it a chance. *It's too hard, someone else is already doing it, it's too complicated, I don't have the right skill set, I don't have time,* and so on.

The truth is, ideas come a dime a dozen, and the only ones that really count are the ones you actually pay attention to, pursue, and try out. This means, if we never made the effort to pursue an idea, we can't cry over what we didn't accomplish because we didn't do anything in the first place. (Excuse me again, while I check myself for those wasted tears I just shed!)

Ideas can come to you randomly, like getting an "*aha moment*" on how to solve a problem you constantly face but could never find a good solution for. They can come to you in the shower or while you are exercising—two scenarios when you have fewer distractions so your mind has a greater opportunity to get creative. Your ideas can come to you from thinking about the talents and passions you have, or from someone else bringing a problem or opportunity to your attention, or from sitting down for an intentional brainstorming session.

I can relate to all of the above. For me personally, my best ideas come to me in the shower when I'm belting it out loud, completely out of tune, and feeling super-relaxed (*Ding! Ding! Ding!* That's how the name "Clever Girl Finance" came about!), from my girlfriends telling me, "*Hey, girl, you should try out XYZ,*" and from making time for those aforementioned intentional brainstorming sessions (which I'll cover more in a minute).

One thing to keep in mind is that your business ideas don't *have* to be tied to your passions. Yes, in many instances, this is the case, and it's great to pursue your passions—but it's also perfectly fine to start a business if it's tied to your skillset or past experiences or if you simply have an interest in it. What's even more important than passion is commitment: having the determination and follow-through to do what it takes to make your business successful.

Once you've put yourself in the mental space where you are ready to start or scale your side hustle, start listening to your flashes of inspiration. Anytime a random idea comes to you, write it down. Even if you don't act on it right away, writing it down will put it on your list of contenders that you can revisit and explore in more detail later on. No matter how long it takes you to get back to these ideas, writing them down is key. I've forgotten so many ideas I've had simply because I didn't write them down. So now, I make sure that whenever an idea comes to me, I write it down, and when I revisit it later, I'm always glad I made a note of it.

How to Intentionally Brainstorm Your Business Ideas

When it comes to brainstorming and fleshing out your business ideas, it's all about ensuring you do it effectively so you can ensure you've done your due diligence before deciding whether to pursue the ideas. Here are a few key steps to help you get started:

- **Start by compiling your idea list.** You may already have one started, but if not, try to look back through your memories and experiences for any past ideas you've thought of. It's okay for them to be very simple at this stage; you'll make them more detailed as you go through the rest of the brainstorming steps below.

- **Go down your idea list one by one.** It's a good idea to brainstorm your ideas one by one so you can stay focused without getting confused or overwhelmed. If you haven't already, clearly describe what your ideas are and then select one to brainstorm first before moving on to other ideas.

- **Make time.** Making time to brainstorm is just as important as making time to actually work on your side hustle. You may only need a single session, or you might need a series of sessions to really get clear on your idea. Take as much time as you need until you feel confident about your idea. Be sure to choose a location with minimal distractions. Get your paper, notebook, or whiteboard. Turn off your phone, get your cup of tea or coffee, light your scented candle. Essentially, create a brainstorming environment where you'll feel most creative.

- **Ask yourself questions.** Asking questions helps you develop your ideas. Why are you interested in or passionate about this idea? What is the real problem you've identified? How does your initial idea help solve it? Who is your target market? What will you need to execute your idea? Questions like this will really help you get clear on whether or not your idea is something you want to follow through with. If you do decide to pursue the idea, the answers to all of these questions will play a part in the business plan you'll create.

- **Do initial research and look at real-life examples.** Thanks to the internet, you can pretty much find examples of anything and everything. So, type your business ideas into Google search to see what related solutions are (or aren't) already out there. This simple exercise could even lead you to a fresh set of ideas.

- **Ask for feedback.** As you fine-tune your idea, don't be shy to ask your friends and family for feedback. I will, however, caution against only seeking feedback from friends and family who you know will see your vision and support you. While these types of friends and family may be eager to give you feedback, be mindful of the fact that their feedback might be biased because they love you and may not want to hurt your feelings. One way to get around this is to simply say you are asking for a friend! Unless you give it away, this approach typically works well. (It also filters out the people who might just be negative because they don't want to see you succeed.) You can also ask your potential future customers or clients what they think of your idea.

- **Take a break, and then revisit your idea.** Once you've done your initial brainstorming, take a break and come back to review it later. By stepping away and clearing your mind for a while, you might come back to it with some fresh insights or different perspectives that could help you improve your idea.

As you brainstorm, your ideas will become clearer and you'll get a sense of necessary next steps and decisions to make. You can brainstorm solo or with a friend or business partner. Ultimately, your goal is to gain clarity and direction.

Examples of Business Ideas and Popular Niches

Since we are on the topic of ideas, here are some examples of business ideas that can be executed regardless of the industry or niche you are focused on:

- Create and sell physical products or services, e.g., by starting an ecommerce website or opening a brick-and-mortar store.
- Create and sell digital products online, e.g., books, guides, courses, etc.
- Coach, teach, or consult for a fee based on a skill set or expertise you have (credentials may be required depending on the field).
- Become an affiliate for a reputable product or service and get commissions on sales you refer (no pyramid schemes, please!)

In addition, some of the most popular niches to start a side hustle include:

- Health and wellness (e.g., fitness, nutrition)
- Food and beverage (e.g., baking, catering)
- Technology services (e.g., website development, graphic design)
- Beauty and style (e.g., skincare, makeup, hair products, fashion)
- Personal improvement and education (e.g., coaching, consulting, teaching, speaking)

Niches that are typically recession-proof during economic downturns, especially when focused on staples rather than optional luxuries, include:

- Technology and IT
- Food and beverage
- Health services
- Legal services
- Financial services
- Repair or maintenance services
- Baby essentials
- Childcare services

Do you already have some ideas churning in your mind? If so and you are feeling inspired, pause here and get to brainstorming! Taking action when you are feeling most inspired is a great way to keep your momentum going.

Take Action

1. **Write down your ideas.** Get a dedicated business journal or notes section on your phone or computer and commit to writing down any ideas you get, regardless of what they are.
2. **Do a brainstorming session.** Take some time to do some intentional brainstorming on any business ideas you come up with. Don't dismiss them until you've got a chance to think them through.

DOING YOUR RESEARCH: GOOGLE IS YOUR FRIEND

As you start to think through your ideas, seek out resources, and grow your business, remember: Google is your friend! Whenever you begin something new or are ready to take things to the next level, there will be things you don't know. However, that should not be an excuse for not starting or making progress. The internet is such a powerful resource, and it's more than likely that whatever you don't know, you can leverage an online search to get the information you need to get started. It's all about making time and being intentional about doing the research to find the answers you need.

However, it can be overwhelming to cut through all the noise and find the resources you really need, especially when you get thousands of results on even the simplest of online searches. I'm sure you can relate to performing a Google search and getting back a ton of information, half of which isn't useful or doesn't make sense!

So how do you research effectively to take advantage of the power of Google? Here are three key tips to help you get started:

- **Use specific keywords.** In order to find what you need, it helps to be as specific as possible. That's where keywords (or key phrases) come in. Using specific words can help fine-tune the results you get back from your search and save you a ton of time.

- The more specific your keyword choices are, the better your results will be. For example, there's a big difference between searching for "Business plan template" (general) versus "Business plan template for web design company" (specific). The same goes for "How to use Google Sheets" versus "How to create a Google Sheets formula for *XYZ*" The more general keywords will return broader search results, which means you'll get a ton of information to wade through that could take forever. On the other hand, the more specific keywords will get you closer to what you really need.

- **Narrow your search results.** One great way to narrow down your Google results is to leverage the sorting function provided after search results are returned. You can narrow the results down from "All" to have Google only show you "Videos," "Images," or "News," etc. as it relates to your search topic.

Google.com screenshot by author

■ **Add favorite resources to your browser bookmarks.** As you find the search results that are most relevant to what you need, bookmark them! Imagine spending hours doing research on something and going through tons of information only to find later that you can't find the content you wanted to have for future reference. A great way to avoid this annoyance is to create a folder on your browser toolbar and bookmark the various resources you want to revisit. You can even take things an extra step and organize your folders by category of research.

■ Not sure how to create a folder in your bookmarks bar? Do a keyword search for, "How to create a bookmarks folder on *[insert browser name]*" and *voilà!* You can use a simple spreadsheet to track your favorite resources as well. For example, make a column with the website name, a column with the link, and a column with a short summary of what the resource covers.

Research can take time, but it is an extremely important step as you work on your business and fine-tune your products and services. By leveraging these tips, you can do your research more effectively and save yourself valuable time.

ESTABLISHING YOUR BUSINESS VISION AND MISSION

Once you've got your ideas in place, two really important pieces of building a successful business are your business vision and mission, both of which should align with your values and what's meaningful to you as an individual. So, let's get clear on what each one really means.

The *Oxford English Dictionary* defines vision as "the ability to think about or plan the future with imagination and wisdom."[1] Establishing your vision is essentially determining what dreams and goals you ultimately want to achieve and laying out a plan to accomplish them without placing any limitations on your potential. This idea of establishing a vision can be applied to any aspect of your life, including your side hustle. As you think about yours, try to write a vision statement to outline your long-term vision. For example, our vision statement at Clever Girl Finance is: "Empower women to pursue and achieve their dreams of financial wellness in order to live life on their own terms."

Your business *mission* is similar to your business vision, but it focuses on what you want to accomplish today and in the immediate short-term time frame ahead of you—for instance, the next one to five years. It is based on your overall business objective and your approach to reaching that objective. Your business mission translates into your mission statement, which is typically a short sentence that encapsulates your objective. You'll often see mission statements on the "about us" pages of business websites. Using Clever Girl Finance as an example again, our mission statement is to "Provide the right education, products, and services for women to become financially successful, minimizing the impact of any socioeconomic barriers limiting them."

It's not uncommon to see vision and mission statements that are blended together or extremely similar to each other, especially in large companies, but you'll find that these blended statements encompass both their current and future goals and objectives.

But why should having a business vision and mission even matter to you if you're just building a side hustle? Well, regardless of the type of business you are building and no matter how small you are starting out, having a defined vision and mission is essentially your business "why." And as mentioned earlier, having a "why" is what will keep you focused and motivated

---

[1]https://www.lexico.com/definition/vision

to ultimately achieve your goals. Side hustle or not, it's a good idea to have both a long-term vision and a current mission for your business.

Crafting Your Business Vision Statement

To get clear about your business vision, think long-term, focusing on success, and on the big dreams you imagine coming true for your business. Don't worry about what you don't know yet; you'll figure it out along the way. Focus on thinking big!

Crafting Your Mission Statement

To craft your mission statement, think about your immediate business objectives, including who your business is for and how it will positively impact your customers and/or your community, and how you intend to accomplish those objectives.

Both your mission and vision statement will tie into your business plan, which will help you set the stage for the awesome side hustle you are building. We'll get into that in the next chapter!

Take Action

- **Craft your business vision and mission statements.** Using the suggestions in this section, work on crafting your business vision and mission statements. Keep in mind that as your side hustle evolves, and as you learn and grow, you may change these statements to stay in line with your goals and values, and that is perfectly fine. It's also perfectly fine for these statements to be short and sweet.
- **Stay ambitious.** Dream big and don't limit your vision. Leverage your immediate mission to create an actionable approach to achieving your ultimate vision.
- **Keep your personal values in mind.** Ultimately, whatever business you create, you want it to be in line with your values as an individual, which in turn will keep you excited to work on it.

MEET VICKII ONABOLU

Vickii is the founder and CEO of Ermioni's Bake Shop (www .ermionisbakeshop.com). She loves desserts but never had any intention of turning that passion into a business; she simply wanted to bake new things and share them with friends. Her hobby and love of desserts, however, ended up becoming a part-time hustle and then a full-time business, something she's exceedingly proud of. Her biggest pride is hearing the amazing feedback about her cakes and seeing the reactions on people's faces on the rare occasion when she's attending an event where her cakes are being served.

You started a baking business as a part-time side hustle. How did you come up with the idea?

I have always loved desserts and all things sweet. Many, many years ago, before red velvet was the commonplace flavor that it is today, there was only one bakery in London that made red velvet cupcakes. I had heard about them and wanted to taste them, but the bakery wasn't nearby. So, I found a recipe and made my own, and shared them with friends. I really loved American-style baking; layer cakes, cupcakes, cookies. . .and again, these weren't common in London at the time, so I baked my own and always shared them. One of these friends had an engagement party and asked if I'd make her celebration cupcakes. So, I did, only charging her the cost of the materials. At the party, everyone kept asking if I baked as a business and if they could order. I explained that I only did it for fun for friends. However, after a few more of these events happened, I started saying "yes" instead of "no," thinking there was no harm, as nobody was likely to order. But they did, and so Ermioni's Bake Shop was born.

What were some of the first things you did to get your home-based business off the ground?

I attended a bakery course at the beginning that gave really good information on what I needed to do to register my business. It explained, for example, the differences between registering as a Sole Proprietor or a Limited Liability Company. So, I did my research and set up all the legal aspects of the business. I found out what qualifications I needed in order to serve food and registered my baking premises. I then researched bank accounts to find one with a free introductory period and then a minimal charge thereafter. Being a bakeshop, it was important to me that all of my baked goods were incredibly delicious, so a lot of initial research went into recipes—testing various ones and finding the right ones. I also looked into other similar bakeries and saw what their offerings were in order to help me choose how many different types of products to offer. I then researched suppliers for what I would need. For instance, cake tins and boxes, baking ingredients such as flour, sugar, chocolate, and so on.

How did you establish the confidence to charge for your baked goods, especially with friends and family?

I didn't have much confidence to charge properly for a very long time—it really was a process for me to charge what my products were worth. I started off charging friends and family only the cost of the baked goods, with no profit for myself. But as most of my initial customers were friends and family, I found myself spending all my spare time baking and not earning anything for my time. So, I started charging something very minimal on top of the cost and did this for a long time. Then I researched what similar established bakeries were charging and undercut them by a large margin because I didn't feel I could charge anything close to what an established company was charging. This was not because I didn't feel like my cakes were as good, but because I thought nobody would pay a one-woman band the same price as a chain of bakeries.

It was only after a year or so, when I kept being told "Wow, this is so much better than (insert famous London bakery name here)!" that I realized that it didn't matter how small I was—I should be charging what my products were worth and also make baking worth my time. I raised my prices, and since then, I have stood behind my prices, which are on par with the cake market. I'm okay letting customers who don't want to pay my price go. Some people will always try to pay less than you're worth, but I have never had a customer walk away when I've stood firm and refused to reduce my price for them.

What has been most rewarding about your business?

I'm currently on maternity leave; however, for two years, I was running my baking business full-time. The most rewarding thing about this has been the flexibility to manage my days, business, and life by and for myself! I love being my own boss. It has also been really fulfilling to have the opportunity to follow my passion, and I don't take for granted that I have been able to do so.

How did you balance working full-time while running your business and now with a baby?

While I was working full-time, I ran my business in the evenings and on weekends. Fortunately, my job was mostly 9–5. Whilst I had the time in the evenings and weekends to spend working on my business, I wanted to give it as much as I could so I could grow it. I think it is extremely important to live a life you love, and that was my ultimate "why" for working full time and running a side hustle at the same time. I tried to put as many systems in place as possible so I could have a more predictable schedule. For instance, asking clients to order at least a couple of weeks in advance to have the best chance of my having availability. And when I occasionally had a quiet weekend, I did as much prep work as possible for upcoming orders, such as baking cake layers in advance and freezing them. I also would keep some days sacred where I wouldn't take orders so I could enjoy holidays and occasions such as Christmas and days to spend time with family.

What advice would you give anyone in the process of starting or already running their side hustle?

I think my most important piece of advice would be to do something you love and are passionate about, as it isn't easy doing two different jobs; at least one of those should be for more than just the money. However, also make sure your side hustle is worth your time and you are being paid what you deserve. If you are going to sacrifice time that could be spent living life, it should be for a purpose.

CHAPTER 3

Your
Business Plan

The foundation of your side hustle's success starts with a plan.

CREATING A BUSINESS PLAN THAT MAKES SENSE TO YOU

So, let's talk about your business plan! Yup, even with a side hustle, it's important to have a strategy in place for your business, and that's what your business plan is all about. Whether your business is brand-new or tenured, having a laid-out plan will provide you with a roadmap of actionable steps. By creating this plan, you'll get to really assess your business idea and determine what you want to ultimately accomplish. It's an important step, because going through the process of creating a business plan can potentially help you avoid making costly mistakes with your hard-earned money.

Having a business plan is also essential if you need to pivot or make adjustments in the way you plan to run your business or with the products and services you offer. In this scenario, you'd be able to easily look at your existing strategy and take an objective assessment of where you need to make changes. For instance, as a result of the COVID-19 pandemic that impacted every aspect of life in 2020, many business owners had to adjust the way they ran their businesses to accommodate for the health precautions necessary for everyone to stay safe. You could also decide to make a pivot or adjustment due to a shifting economy, changing your business model, adjusting your ideal customer, or simply because you've chosen to take your business in a different direction.

If you are navigating a busy full-time job, family, and/or other life obligations, the idea of creating a business plan might feel daunting. Business plans typically have lots of pages full of tons of information, so creating one could very easily become a huge time suck. Due to the popular (yet misleading) idea that a business plan has to be this incredibly lengthy document, a lot of business owners make the mistake of creating a business plan just for the sake of creating one, packing it full of irrelevant information never to be reviewed again.

Why do people do this? Often, they feel that in order to create a good business plan, it only makes sense to mimic a big, successful company. So, they do a Google search and end up finding a publicly available business plan from a massive company with thousands of products, services, and employees, and use this large company's plan as the template to craft their own. What typically happens with this approach is that the business owner ends up getting extremely frustrated and overwhelmed—#throwthewholebusinessplanaway—and may give up before they even give their business a chance because they got permanently stuck in this planning phase. The exercise ends up being a complete (and unnecessary) waste of precious time.

At the early stages of a business, leveraging the plan of a massive company that has been around for decades is more confusing than it is helpful, simply because your business is at a completely different stage. Your business plan does not need to be a thousand-page document. Nor does it need to be a hundred-page document. It can simply be a few pages that map out the details of your business in a way that makes sense to you. Consider your business plan an ongoing work in progress that helps you map out your path as you work on your business. You can adjust that path as necessary as you change or improve your products and services, learn more about your audience, and grow your business. It's essentially your business blueprint that you revisit often to ensure you are on the right path with your long-term business goals.

What to Include in Your Business Plan

So, with all of that being said, what exactly should you have in your business plan? Well, like I mentioned, you want to create a plan that makes sense to you and that you can easily review. Whether it's long or short (totally up to you), here are some key things you should consider including in your plan and some questions to consider that can help during the process. Keep in mind, we'll be delving into all these key things in more detail along the way in this book.

- **What your business is about.** Just as it sounds, this is essentially you outlining exactly what your business does. This would be the place where you include your business vision and mission statement (which we went over earlier). To get clear on this section, start by answering the question, "What pain point does my target audience have, and how do I intend to solve it with this business?"

- **What your legal entity will be.** You'll also want to ensure that your business is set up correctly, both legally and tax-wise. This is where the structure of your business comes into play. Is your business going to be a sole proprietorship, partnership, limited liability company (LLC), or perhaps even a corporation?

- **Who your business is for.** Who do you imagine being your ideal customer on a recurring basis? You'll want to identify who they are, including things like where they're located, their age, their income, and why they would be interested in your business.

- **The products and/or services you plan to offer.** What products and services do you plan on offering? Are they in line with the problem your business will be solving? It's also a good idea to start thinking about how you will price your products or services in this section.

- **Your competition/what already exists.** No business plan is complete without some rough ideas about your competition. Where is your competition located? What are the strengths and weaknesses of their offering? And of course, how can you differentiate yourself from them and make your offering better? The more you understand your competition and what exists in your space, the better positioned you are to find opportunities to make your business stand out from the crowd.

- **Your plan to promote your business.** How and where will you be selling your products and services? How do you intend to engage and attract your ideal customer? This will tie into how you leverage social media, your website, your brand, and other avenues to effectively generate sales.

- **Your business finances.** Having a firm handle on your business finances is key to building a successful and profitable business. Have you identified what your startup costs will be? What about your monthly recurring expenses? How much would you need to earn at a minimum each month to break even and then become profitable? These are all business finance questions you want to start thinking about.

- **Your business goals.** The same way you have goals for your personal life, you should set goals for your business. Basically, what do you want to get done, and by when? Be sure to include revenue goals and break your goals down weekly, monthly, quarterly, and annually. Don't overwhelm yourself with too many things to do at once. Instead, stick to three to five main goals and add on as you accomplish them.

- **How you will manage your business.** How much time can you dedicate each day toward working on your business? What will your schedule look like? What help will you need? It's important to determine how much time you can dedicate to growing your business and the kind of help you think you'll need, e.g., social media management, packing, and shipping, customer outreach, etc. This will help you set clear objectives and deadlines around what you need to get done.

Laying out all of these pieces will help set the foundation for a solid business plan and strategy that can guide you and give you clarity around making your business decisions. Remember that it's not about how long your document is; it's about creating a useful plan to help you build the business you desire!

Take Action

It's time to work on creating or adjusting your business plan!

- If you've never created a business plan, leverage the key pieces highlighted in the "what to include" section of this chapter to create your plan.

- If you already have a business plan written, pull it out, dust it off, and determine what you need to do to adjust it if necessary, to make sure it serves your current needs and helps you accomplish your business vision.

- Be sure to include:

  - What your business is about
  - What your legal entity will be
  - Who your business is for
  - The products and/or services you plan to offer
  - Your plan to promote your business
  - Your competition/what already exists
  - Your business finances
  - Your business goals
  - How you will manage your business

WHAT LEGAL STRUCTURE DO YOU NEED?

When you initially had your amazing idea to start a business, the last thing that was probably on your mind was anything related to a legal question, right? Determining your legal responsibilities as a business owner and determining exactly how to set up your business legally is likely to be the least exciting part of starting and building a business.

However, when it comes to your business, even if it's just a side hustle, the legal aspect of your business isn't something that you can just ignore. This is because if you sell a product or service, the government considers you a business even if you haven't registered it. Thus, it makes sense to ensure that you have things set up the right way for your business so you can avoid any issues in the future.

I reached out to my friend Ayesha Chidolue, managing attorney at the Chidolue Law Firm, PLLC (www.chidoluelaw.com), where she practices business, trademark and immigration law, to talk about the importance of having the right legal structure in place regardless of whether it's a side hustle or not. Here's what she said:

> As a business owner, it is important to separate the liability of your business from your own personal liability. This is because when it comes to any business debt, when there is no separate entity, you tend to have greater financial liability and responsibility to others and the majority of the time, most business owners, especially small business owners cannot afford the higher liability that comes with owning a business. So, no matter how small you think your side hustle is, you should still consider getting it incorporated into either an LLC or a corporation as they will both provide you with Limited Liability Protection.

Ayesha also explains the implications that business owners need to be aware of if they don't have the right business structure in place and the importance of hiring a business lawyer if necessary:

> In terms of implications, the biggest drawback is being sued and the court finds you liable for the financial payment. At this point, there is no corporate veil of protection. This means you will be directly sued as an individual and will personally be responsible for any financial judgment. However, if you were a legal structure, your business will be responsible and as long as you don't co-mingle your personal and business finances, they won't come after your personal assets. Another key implication with not setting up a legal structure is that you might miss out on business

opportunities with other interested partners who prefer to work with people who have a legal structure. There is a saying that goes, "Penny wise, pound foolish." A lot of times, side hustlers or smaller businesses don't believe they need a business attorney until something actually happens in their business. However, this is the wrong thought process. Hiring an attorney from the onset of your business can help you avoid a lot of costly mistakes in the long run. Not only can they help you with structuring your business and tax designation correctly, but they can also advise you on valuable intellectual property protections and the standard contracts and agreements that each business should have. When you have all these in place from the beginning, you can potentially save several thousands of dollars when an issue arises.

To help you decide what might work best for you, let's get into the different business structures. Keep in mind that even if you have an existing business, you can still adjust your business structure.

Types of Business Structures

There are different types of business structures to choose from, including a sole proprietorship, partnership, limited liability company (LLC), or corporation. Things can start to get a little confusing here, so I'll break each one down. The four main business structures (or entities, as they are sometimes called) are:

1. **Sole proprietorship.** A sole proprietorship is the easiest business structure to form. As a matter of fact, you are automatically considered to be a sole proprietorship if you do business activities, even if you don't officially register as a business. With this type of business structure, your business assets and liabilities are not separated from your personal assets and liabilities.[1] This means that you

---

[1] https://www.sba.gov/business-guide/launch-your-business/choose-business-structure

are personally responsible for all liabilities related to your business. And by *liability*, I'm referring specifically to any obligations that arise from your business, whether financial or otherwise.[2]

2. **Partnership.** As the name implies, in a partnership you run your business with a partner or multiple partners (aka owners), and your business is run and managed based on a partnership agreement you decide upon. A partnership can be set up as a limited partnership (LP) where one general partner has unlimited liability while other partners have limited liability (and also limited control) based on the partnership agreement you create. They can also be set up as a limited liability partnership (LLP), where every partner has limited liability. An LLP protects each partner against the actions of other partners and against any business debts held against the company.[3] If you are starting a business with a business partner, a partnership structure would be best suited for you.

3. **Limited liability company (LLC).** A limited liability company (LLC) protects you from personal liability for any debts or claims made against your business. This means your personal assets like your car, home, savings, investments, and assets would not be at risk if your business were to face a lawsuit or bankruptcy. Profits and losses are tied to your personal income and you are not subject to corporate taxes, even though the liability protection offered by an LLC is similar to that of a corporation. With an LLC, you can also have co-owners (similar to a partnership) who are called members. LLCs are great for any higher-risk businesses (e.g., offering high-cost or extensive products and services), or for

---

[2]https://capital.com/liability-definition
[3]https://www.sba.gov/business-guide/launch-your-business/choose-business-structure

business owners that have personal assets that need to be protected.[4] Personally, I think an LLC is a great option for most business owners. Protecting your personal assets is important, and it's something a sole proprietorship does not offer. If you are a licensed professional, depending on your state requirement, you may be required to form a professional limited liability company (PLLC). A PLLC is a business entity designed for licensed professionals, such as lawyers, doctors, architects, engineers, accountants, and chiropractors.[5]

4. **Corporation.** With a corporation, your business is a completely separate legal entity and only the entity itself is legally responsible for any liabilities. In the United States, the IRS views a corporation as an individual taxpayer, which means the corporation will pay corporate income tax. If shareholders (corporation owners) are paid dividends or salaries, they would also be subject to income tax, which means a double taxation effect. That said, there are also benefits to corporations. They have limited liability (as previously mentioned), the ability to raise capital by selling shares, and the ability for the corporation to continue existence even if the original founders are no longer there.[6] Corporations can further be broken down based on the specific features they have.

- **C Corp.** A C Corp is a standard corporation, also known as a regular corporation. If a C Corp is sued, the personal assets of its shareholders are not at risk, unlike with a partnership or sole proprietorship.

---

[4]https://www.sba.gov/business-guide/launch-your-business/choose-business-structure
[5]https://www.nolo.com/legal-encyclopedia/what-professional-limited-liability-company.html
[6]https://www.inc.com/encyclopedia/c-corporation.html

- **S Corp.** This type of corporation does not pay any federal income taxes and instead passes all income, losses, and deductions directly to the shareholders. An S Corp is usually a small corporation where the owners are also the shareholders.[7]

- **B Corp.** Although they are for-profit corporations, B corporations focus on accountability and transparency, and are driven by their mission and not just profits. They agree to be held accountable for their level of social and environmental responsibility, and must meet specific requirements to be certified as a B Corp.

- **Nonprofit corporation.** These are corporations focused on education, charity, religion, or other types of work that benefit a community, demographic, or the general public. A nonprofit status allows them to be exempt from state or federal taxes on any profits they make. Profits are used to pay their staff and further the work they do.

Which Business Structure Is Right for You?

The type of business structure you set up has little to do with the amount of time you spend working on your business (i.e., side hustle vs. full-time business), and more to do with how you intend to run and fund your business as well as the liability protection and other benefits you want for your business. Keep in mind that you can also change your business structure as your business grows.

As you think through what the best legal structure is for your business needs, two invaluable resources to guide you on your entrepreneurial journey are the business and taxation sections of your state government website (find your state government

---

[7]https://www.yourdictionary.com/s-corporation#:~:text=The%20definition%20of%20an%20S,founders%20are%20also%20the%20shareholders,

website at irs.gov and search "state government websites") and the US Small Business Administration website (sba.gov).

These resources go into specific detail regarding the business structures mentioned in this section. They also include the pros and cons of each, as well as the specific steps you need to take to set up your business under any of these structures.

Don't Forget Your Federal Employer Identification Number

As you set up your business structure, one additional thing to think about is obtaining your Federal Employer Identification Number, also typically abbreviated to EIN. This is your business tax ID that the IRS may require you to have depending on the business structure you've selected. Your EIN is essentially like your Social Security number but is specifically for your business. It ties into your business tax filings, hiring employees, and other important and required legalities for your business.

If you are a sole proprietor or an LLC with no employees, an EIN is optional, not required. I'd recommend you get one anyway so you don't have to put your Social Security number on forms and applications. It's always a good idea to minimize your risk of identity theft, especially in this day and age.

Applying for Your EIN

Obtaining an EIN can be done through a completely free service offered by the IRS (so beware of anyone trying to charge you for it!). Just visit IRS.gov and search "How to apply for an EIN." It's a very straightforward process and all you need to do is follow the instructions.

If you have questions or need help determining your business legal structure beyond what the resources mentioned in this section provide, you can speak with a business accountant or lawyer to help guide you.

NOTE

If you are outside the United States, be sure to do specific research to learn how each of these and other legal entities are structured in your country and what their potential tax implications are.

Take Action

- Take some time to decide on a business structure that will work best for your type of business, paying specific attention to liability protection. (I'd definitely recommend an LLC or that you eventually convert to an LLC once you get your business up and running.)
- Be sure to leverage the resources provided in the business and taxation sections of your state government website (visit irs.gov and search "state government websites") and the US Small Business Administration website (sba.gov). They offer excellent insights and guidance for most questions business owners have.
- Apply for your Federal Employer Identification Number if you haven't already by going to IRS.gov and searching "How to apply for an EIN.

WHO IS YOUR BUSINESS FOR, AND WHY SHOULD THEY BUY FROM YOU?

One of the most important components for building a successful business is truly understanding who your ideal customer is and why they should buy from you. As a business owner, you obviously want to grow your business, become profitable, and leverage the money you make to pursue your life goals. But being able to achieve any of this is based on your ability to sell your products and services. After all, you've created your business to sell your products and services to this ideal customer.

A big mistake many business owners make is overlooking their actual customers and instead focusing solely on the products and services that they are trying to sell, without taking into consideration who is going to buy them. However, the truth is, regardless of what your products or services are, you ultimately need someone to buy them, and that "someone" is your ideal customer. Since your success relies on getting customers, it makes sense to really focus on understanding who your target customers are and their motivations to purchase from you.

When it comes to purchase motivation, the main reason people will buy from your business is because you are helping them solve a problem. For instance, depending on your business niche, it could be a mom looking for the perfect cake for her child's first birthday, a business that needs to improve their outdated website design, or an individual wanting to achieve their health or career goals.

People will come to you to solve their problem because of your expertise, or if they think your product is better or has a higher perceived value than that of your competitors. When a customer chooses to buy from your business, your goal is to make them happy about their experience and with their purchase. Ultimately, the product or service you offer through your business becomes their problem-solver and delivers an amazing experience. If done right, your customers are likely to return, make repeat purchases, and, very importantly, tell other people (aka new potential customers) about your business as well.

However, in order for you to get that first purchase that leads to a happy customer, that potential customer needs to feel that you understand their needs. This means establishing a connection with them where you showcase exactly how your business can solve their problems. And in order to establish this connection, you need to know exactly who your ideal customer is and how to reach them!

For example, let's take a look at the cosmetics brand Fenty Beauty, which I absolutely love. They are an amazing beauty company founded by musician, actress, and businesswoman Rihanna. One of the reasons why Fenty Beauty is such a successful company is because of its cosmetics line that truly caters to all skin tones. For me as a new customer who had faced this problem for years, these products were a Godsend.

From the moment I started wearing makeup, finding the right foundation that perfectly suited my skin tone was always an issue. The options provided by mainstream brands were limited, and even when my skin tone was catered to, the colors were just never right. As a result, I would find myself mixing and matching different products just to get my perfect shade. When Fenty Beauty came onto the scene with a whopping 40 variations of foundation shades, compared to the average 5 or 6 that other brands made, I was instantly drawn to purchase the products.

Another reason for its success is its compelling mission that focuses on inclusivity and diversity in beauty, showcasing models of all ethnic backgrounds, which is also extremely meaningful to me as a consumer of the products. It definitely helped that the brand had the celebrity star power of Rihanna, but the products spoke for themselves: high-quality, beautifully branded, and showcased by a variety of women, including women who looked like me. Once I tried it, I was sold and have continued to purchase from the brand ever since.

As a company, Fenty Beauty is clear about its target audience, and I am part of that target audience. I had a specific problem with finding the right foundation, and the products solved my problem. Whenever anyone asks me for a foundation recommendation, I mention Fenty Beauty among my favorites. The way I feel about Fenty Beauty is how you want your customers to feel about your business.

So, I'll ask you now, who is your target audience?

Another big mistake that business owners make is creating a business that caters to everyone, because they feel their product is universal and can be used by anyone. While it is certainly possible for your product to be broadly appealing and useful, it can get confusing for you to determine who you are trying to reach if you don't have a target audience in mind. Plus, it can be even more confusing for potential customers to determine if your product is a right fit for them.

For example, if you have an event planning business and your website lists every event type under the sun—parties, corporate events, sporting events, religious events, seminars and conferences, trade shows, galas, workshops, etc.—alongside a mishmash of photos, who are you really attracting? If a potential bride looking for a wedding planner came across your website and saw this extensive list of every event type, it would give her pause. If she doesn't see anything specific that lets her know your business is right for her, she's likely to exit your website and forget all about you in a matter of seconds. And if she lingered to give it more thought, she might wonder if you were truly an expert in your field and whether you'd even be capable of creating the wedding of her dreams. Without having real clarity on who you plan events for, it will be really difficult to attract your ideal customer.

On the flipside, imagine if this bride came to your website and saw immediately that you specialized in planning weddings and parties, and saw a variety of specific photos and videos from weddings you've planned. Then imagine that she read through your customer testimonials, reviewed your service list, which ties into what she needs, and then clicked on your Instagram profile that showcases even more amazing images of the weddings you've planned. You'd be one step closer to having her fill out a consultation form and potentially booking you for her big day.

This example illustrates the importance of why you need to really get clear on who your customer is.

How to Get Clear on Your Ideal Customer

When it comes to identifying your ideal customer, creating a "customer avatar" can be extremely helpful. Your customer avatar is basically a detailed profile that represents the person that you'd want to buy your products and services. It's the person you are trying to get to know, so you can create products and services that serve their needs and solve their specific problems with a positive outcome. Think of creating a customer avatar like starting a new relationship with someone you want to get to know really well.

As you lay out your customer avatar, some things you may want to include are things like their age, gender, marital status, education level, whether they have children, their occupation, income, and location. You could also want to outline their likes and dislikes, where they hang out, what their main pain points are (be it in their life, family, work, etc.), and exactly how your business can solve those pain points.

To narrow things down even further, you can ask yourself questions like:

- "What is my ideal customer trying to accomplish by leveraging my products and services?"
- "Where are they currently getting the information to solve their problems?"
- "What existing brands or companies do they trust?"
- "Why would my business be attractive to them?"
- "What would make them *not* want to purchase from me?"

Depending on your type of business, you can have more than one customer avatar. Keep in mind, though, that the whole idea behind creating these avatars is to ensure that you know exactly who you are trying to reach and you are creating the right products, services, and marketing strategies to reach and help them. Creating too many avatars can be confusing and cause you to lose focus because you are spreading your efforts too thin. Starting with one or two avatars is ideal to give you maximum clarity about your plan to reach your ideal customers.

Keep in mind that as you lay out your avatars, it's okay if you make some assumptions to start. As you learn more about your target audience, you can fine-tune your avatars. In addition, as your products and services evolve and as your business grows, your avatars may change. It's all about ensuring that you continue to speak to your ideal customer; if your ideal customer changes over time, so will your avatars.

By doing this exercise of creating your avatars, you'll be able to craft a specific marketing strategy for your ideal client, which in turn will get you closer to sales—and we're all about that *cha-ching!*

Take Action

Now is a great time to lay out who your ideal customer is by creating your customer avatars, which you can build into the "who your business is for" section of your business plan.

- **Create your avatar(s).** As you create your avatars, be sure to include the key information that is relevant for your specific business. Some suggestions include:
  - Age
  - Gender
  - Marital status
  - Education level
  - Whether they have children
  - Occupation
  - Income
  - Location
  - Their likes and dislikes
  - Where they hang out
  - Their main pain points as it relates to your business
  - Exactly how your business can solve their pain points

- **Fine-tune your customer avatar.** Also, write your answers to the following questions to help you fine-tune your customer avatar:
  - What is my ideal customer trying to accomplish by leveraging my products and services?
  - Where are they currently getting the information to solve their problems?
  - What existing brands or companies do they trust?
  - Why would your business be attractive to them?
  - What would make them *not* want to purchase from me?

Keep the information you gather from this exercise handy, as you'll be referring back to it when you work on your business marketing strategy!

DEFINING YOUR PRODUCTS AND SERVICES

So now you've gotten clear on who your ideal customer is, the next step is to get clear on exactly what you are offering to your customers by way of your products and services. Your products and services are basically your attempt to solve your customers' problem or satisfy their need or want. It doesn't matter if you sell baked goods, household items, beauty and skincare items, coaching or consulting, web design, technology services, healthcare or child care services—these can all be categorized as products or services. The products you offer usually mean physical items, while the services you offer, although non-physical items, refer to the actions you take to meet your customers' needs.

Getting clear on your products and services will help you properly describe what it is you are selling and in turn fine-tune the way you communicate to your customer about your ability to meet their needs, encouraging them to buy from you. You'll develop your marketing approach based on two things: who you help and what your business offers.

How to Define What You Are Selling

Start by laying out the specific products and services you'll be selling. What exactly are they? I recommend simply starting out with one or two products or services, instead of offering many all at once. Starting small will give you the opportunity to really focus on your initial offering, test it out on your audience, make adjustments, and ensure that you have the right product–market fit, i.e., the right products or services that satisfy your ideal customers' needs. Once you've accomplished this with your first few products, you can expand your offerings to leverage the new insights you've gained. If your test is unsuccessful, you can quickly move on to the next product or service you want to test with your ideal customer—again, leveraging the valuable insights you've gained.

Having too many products or services right away can be confusing to manage and make measuring their individual successes and outcomes difficult. Especially when you consider everything else that goes into running your business, you don't want to overwhelm yourself.

Value First, Product Second

As you think through your products and services, you want to keep in mind that whatever your offerings are, they should add value and meet your customers' needs. For example, if you sell books, your customers are buying your books for the knowledge or entertainment they contain, not just for the sake of physically owning a book. (After all, knowledge is why you picked up this particular book, right?) If you sell fitness coaching, your customers are really buying health, not just a workout session. It's easy to get caught up in product ideas and come up with a long list of products and services that you think your customer will like. However, you need to make sure those product ideas align with their pain points, needs, or wants, and also align with what you want your business to be about.

Once you have your products and services laid out, you'll also want to figure out what variations of each specific product or service you'll offer, how you'll price them (we'll be covering pricing your products in the business finances section of this book), and how you'll deliver them. It's also worth considering what forms of payment you'd accept and what return policy or guarantees you'd offer.

With all of this planned out, you can now create your first product or service description, highlighting the value it offers and how exactly your offering will meet your customer's needs. This description will go on your website and will be tied to your social media and marketing efforts.

Remember, as you gain new insights, you can edit and adjust all of this as you feel necessary.

Take Action

In the "products and/or services you plan to offer" section of your business plan, lay out the product and service ideas you have in mind. Here are some questions to help you work through the process:

- What exactly are your products and services?
- What variations of each specific product or service will you offer?
- How will you price each product and service?
- What payments will you accept?
- What return policy or guarantees will you offer?
- What value will your product deliver to your customers?

Based on your responses to these questions, you can then create your product and service descriptions.

ASSESSING YOUR COMPETITION

As you go through this process of laying the right foundations for your business, it's also important to do your research in order to understand what other businesses already exist out there that are similar to yours. The standard term for this approach would be "assessing your competition." The word *competition* can sound aggressive, but as women, we shouldn't be afraid to compete and show our value! When it comes to business, understanding who your competitors are is a great way to get ahead.

If you do your research the right way, you can gain some valuable insights from your competitors. You can learn which of their products and services are working well and which ones aren't. You can study their business mistakes, learn from them, and avoid making similar mistakes in your own business. You can look at their successes and let them motivate you to succeed as well. Plus, you can identify gaps that your competition is not yet filling and use what you learn to differentiate yourself and make your products and services stand out. This is how you leverage competition in a healthy way!

That being said, let's get into how you can assess your competition.

How to Assess Your Competition

When it comes to your competition, even gaining a little bit of insight into how they operate can help you with some key decision-making. Keep in mind, your goal with assessing your competition is to learn from them and gain insights to help you grow your own business. Here are some key steps to help you get started with your assessment:

- **Determine who your competitors are.** When it comes to assessing your competition, the first step is obviously to determine who they are. Specifically, who your *direct* competition is. These are the businesses that currently exist in your space and offer similar products and services that meet your ideal customers' needs. Usually, your direct competitors will be a similar size or slightly larger than your business. Create a list of these competitors as you identify them so you can do a deeper analysis on them later. A top-five list is a great baseline of competitors to start with. As your business grows, this list may change.

- **Take a look at the types of products and services your competitors sell.** This will help you gain insights about what they offer and in what variations. You'll also learn about their pricing structure and how they offer discounts, which can help you assess the quality of their products and services in relation to their pricing. Keep in mind that price is just one of the many reasons that customers choose to buy a product. It all boils down to how valuable they find the product, which could be based on a combination of different factors, including branding and brand perception, the purchase experience, and product quality, among other factors.

- **Understand how they market and sell their products and services.** Looking at your competitors' marketing and sales strategies can help you gain a better understanding of how they acquire their customers. This means understanding the channels they use for marketing and selling, whether they're promoting their business through a blog, via social media platforms like Instagram, Facebook, and Pinterest, by making videos on YouTube, through word-of-mouth referrals in their community, or a combination of all of the above. You also want to know where they have their strongest marketing presence across all the various platforms.

- When it comes to sales, it's similar: you want to understand the specific channels they use to make sales and what their strongest sales channel is, whether it's via their website, a physical location, or through third parties like affiliates and wholesalers. Ultimately, marketing leads to sales, and if there's something that's working well for your competition, you definitely want to know what it is and how you can make it work for you too!

■ **Review their customer experience.** Another great way to assess your competition is to take a look at what their customers are saying. While reviews on the actual competitors' websites are a good start, businesses will typically curate their best reviews to showcase on their own websites (I mean, who wouldn't!). However, by reading the comments on their social posts, searching their popular hashtags, or reading what customers are saying about them on various online forums, you may be able to get a more realistic glimpse of what their average customer experience is like. You can even take your research further and make a purchase to get a sense of the end-to-end experience for yourself as well. A customer's experience is extremely important to your business because a great experience can make them raving evangelists for your business (yes to free marketing!) and a poor experience can cause them to deter other potential customers from buying from you. So, when it comes to your competitors' customer experience, take note of what people are loving, and what they are not.

■ **Determine their strengths, weaknesses, and potential opportunities.** As you go through each of the already mentioned assessment steps, also take note of what your competition does really well (their strengths), what they don't do well or could do better (their weaknesses), and based on this, what opportunities exist for you to differentiate yourself or fill an existing gap. This helps you determine how to better position your business for success.

Lastly, if you're worried about harming other small businesses by competing with them, put those fears to rest. When it comes to competition, there's enough room for everyone to succeed, because ultimately you bring the uniqueness of you to what you do, and no one can replicate that. They'll attract some customers with their specialties, and you'll attract others that prefer what you're offering.

Also note that while it's definitely worthwhile to understand your competitors and how they operate, going overboard can sidetrack you from your goals. Your main focus should be on what *you* ultimately want to accomplish for your business. Keeping an eye on your competition is just one more way to enhance your learning and motivate your success.

Take Action

Assess your competition:

- What similarly sized businesses currently exist in your space that have similar products and services that could meet your ideal customer's needs?
- What products and services do your competitors offer, and at what price?
- How would you describe the value of their product?
- How do they market their products and services, and on what platforms do they have the strongest presence?
- What are the main sales channels they leverage?
- What is their customer experience like?
- Overall, what would you say are your competitors' strengths and weaknesses, and what potential opportunities can you take advantage of to help your business stand out?

Based on this assessment of your existing competition, the next thing you want to do is identify and outline the key things that you can start to implement in your business to deliver an outstanding product or service, convey the value of your brand, and create an amazing purchase experience for your customers. (Next chapter incoming!)

MEET TIWA LAWRENCE

Tiwa is a bridal makeup artist and educator who serves clients in North Carolina and beyond (TiwaLawrence.com). Over the past 15 years, she has had the pleasure of providing luxury bridal makeup services for hundreds of brides and countless amazing women. Her passion for her business stems from giving women impactful makeovers and sharing her knowledge to help other makeup artists make a living doing what they love. Being able to profit doing what she truly loves has been a dream in and of itself.

You have run a successful makeup business for several years now, which you started as a side hustle; what were some key things you had in your business plan that helped you successfully launch and run your business?

I didn't have it all figured out when I started my business, but I didn't let what I didn't know stop me from moving forward with my side hustle. I used that feeling as fuel to learn more about what it would take to succeed and stand out in my market. It is easy to overthink a business plan and overanalyze the entire process. For me, I knew if I overcomplicated the process, it would paralyze me and I would not start! I wanted to make sure I didn't have any excuses and I didn't put any undue pressure on myself (especially with a full-time job and a part-time job in the beauty industry at the time). I decided that my plan didn't have to be something fancy or super-professional. The most important components in the plan just needed to be simple and clear. The plan I created included the following components:

My mission: What did I want to add to this world through my gifts?

My clients: Who would be my clients?

My solutions: What issues would they need me to help them solve (with my strengths, gifts, and expertise)?

My services: The type of services I wanted to provide my clients, to help them solve the issues I mentioned previously.

My workspace: Where would I be working with my clients (would it be in person, at a studio, on-location only, or would I provide value online)?

My visibility and promotion: How would people find out about my business and what marketing would I use to reach those clients?

My team: Who would be doing what in the business? (In the beginning, I was everything in my business and I fulfilled every role in my business.)

My relationships: How did I want to show up in the relationship with my customers and others in the industry/market?

My money: How would I make money in the business, and what would it cost me to run the business (making sure to break down all expenses)?

My rates: I set up my rates/client investment, so that my time, labor, and cost of goods were in line with my ideal client's needs.

Last but not least, an element of time management needed to be added to the plan. Typically, with a side hustle, one might have other commitments, including a job and maybe family obligations. You have to have a plan of how you will manage your time to make sure you are not letting your work suffer at your full-time job (before you quit) and you are using the spare time you have to the best of your ability. This will help you stay focused and prevent you from getting distracted and/or overwhelmed. The funds I made at my full-time job bankrolled my passion and gave me the grace to invest my spare time in my new side hustle. I am thankful for the full-time job I had, because without it. . .I wouldn't have been able to do what I truly loved.

How did you get clear on the clientele you wanted to offer your products and services to?

I started off doing makeup for anyone who had a face on their head, but as time went on, I was able to eliminate and add to the characteristics and traits that I wanted to attract in a client. In the beginning, I found it difficult to let go of clients who were not a good fit for my business, because my natural instinct is to help everyone. Once I was able to figure out and narrow down who my ideal client would be, it made it easier to turn down clients who I knew would not be a good fit for the type of services I wanted to provide.I would say at this point in my career, most of my clientele and income are tied to bridal-related services and education, which is what I wanted. As I started to unpack what I wanted in my business and my lifestyle, I realized that while living in one of the fastest-growing family cities in the country, I would thrive the best working in the bridal industry, as opposed to working in the editorial or TV & Film market. Once I came to that determination, I did an inventory of all the clients I had worked with in the past and I thought through what all my dream clients had in common. From that point on, I coined the term "Dream Bride" to describe this dream client of mine. I was quickly able to pinpoint who my ideal client was, by visualizing and putting a face to this person. I knew she would be discerning and trusting of my services and she would be able to understand why she needed to make an investment in looking her very best for the most important day of her life and how hiring me would help her to achieve that goal. This "Dream Bride" would be someone who valued a clean, polished, and elegant makeup look. I was able to go as far as figuring out where she works, what she loves to do, and what exactly she would need from me on a service level and as an intimate part of her wedding story. This analysis has made it easier to market to and attract my "Dream Bride."

You are consistently busy and have built a name for yourself in your industry among brides and celebrity clients alike. How did you differentiate yourself from your competition at the early stages of your business?

I was reading a blog post by Seth Godin recently, where he said, "The best way to make a hit is to build something for the smallest viable audience and make it so good that people tell their peers."

This really hit home for me because when I started in the makeup artistry game, I wasn't able to articulate what I was doing, but without question, this is exactly what I had the natural inclination to do, which set me apart from others in the industry.

Another thing is that I never looked at others as my competition. The thought never crossed my mind because I was so focused on what I was doing. I was hungry and wanted to keep honing my skills. In fact, some of the other makeup artists in my same market were my biggest allies and supporters when I started (I could write a whole book about how this happened for me). I wanted to reach as many people as possible, and I made sure to give each woman I had the pleasure of working with my full attention, focus, and care. The result was that clients never forgot me. They would return for my services time and time again. But more importantly, they would refer their friends and family members to me repeatedly. Before I knew it, there was a word-of-mouth movement going on in my city. People would leave reviews online and share their experience with my small business, and that helped others looking for bridal makeup services to learn about the type of services I provide. In the early stages of my business, I rarely said no to an opportunity. I built business relationships that are still in place today, which were a huge source of my referrals. I worked very hard on the customer service I provided clients. I have kept this same spirit as I have grown my business. I try my very best never to say no (within reason) when I know myself and the client are a good fit. My goal is to make sure the client is happy with the investment they made when they chose my services, and to add value. I also make sure I am always mentally present when I talk to or deal with my clients, which has been instrumental in building amazing relationships.

With the impact of the 2020 pandemic (COVID-19), like many business owners, you had to pivot and make adjustments. How did you adjust your business plan and approach?
When it came to making adjustments in my plan and approach, the first thing I did was try not to panic. The wedding industry (just like many other industries) has been severely impacted by the pandemic and put a harsh halt to all activities surrounding the most important day in the lives of many couples. I tried to look at the possible positives in the situation despite the fact that the highest-earning activities in my business had to do with in-person interactions. The second thing I did was look over all the bookings I had in place until the end of 2020. My immediate focus was on all my brides who were having to cancel or postpone their weddings. I made sure to provide the best customer service to help to alleviate some of the disappointment and stress they were going through. The next thing I did was update my contracts and administration procedures. I had to make sure I updated my contracts to address COVID-19 and add other options for my brides. I have always been a big advocate for proper sanitation in the makeup industry. This was a perfect time to revisit my sanitation practices to ensure I was doing everything to keep my clients and myself safe. I added additional safety precautions to help protect my clients and myself during makeup sessions. I wanted them to feel safe knowing their safety is my and my team's primary priority. I also added more virtual options for bridal education and makeup lessons. Last but not least, I used the time to network! Networking and relationship building within the wedding industry has always been super-important in building my business. I really worked on building relationships with other wedding vendors in the area. Thank God for Zoom. As a result, I was included as part of some wedding-vendor-related initiatives and panels concerning diversity and

inclusion within the wedding industry. I was able to share my expertise in the wedding industry and share my thoughts and suggestions for improvements during a time of uncertainty, unrest, and racial injustice.

Having a plan for your business has been extremely helpful to you, so what advice would you give someone about the importance of laying out a plan when trying to start or scale their side hustle?

Thinking of my business plan as a "plan for success" is one way I justified the importance of having a business plan. I would be lying if I said starting a side hustle while working a full-time job is easy. It takes a lot of time, sacrifice, and money (depending on the side hustle) to begin. It isn't easy, but starting a side hustle is "simple" enough and anyone can do it. I say simple because the steps are straightforward and with dedication, consistency, focus, and a plan, you can make it work. It is one of the most rewarding things I have ever done in my life. I had a plan of what I wanted out of my side hustle but I didn't have an exact plan for how to quit my full-time job in order to take on my side hustle full-time when I started. However, as I continued on the journey, I realized it was the natural progression that needed to happen. This is what propelled me to create a total plan of action. When you are about to embark on this new journey, there is nothing better than having a plan. Be it a Plan A or a Plan B or Plan C or even a Plan Z. Nine times out of ten, if your plans A or B are solid, you never have to move past those two options. But if you have to, no sweat. . .you already have a Plan C. Having a plan helps to keep you focused. I was lucky enough not to have many distractions when it came to social media or all the many courses, training, podcasts, and other sources of information that are out there now. In the world today, a lot more focus is needed to stay on track. It is easy to get derailed when one is seeing what others in the same industry or field are doing. Having a plan helps to keep you on track and keeps you from succumbing to these distractions.

Scaling a side hustle means you are at a place where you know what you want and your business is making an impact and consistent income. The plan you create will be your blueprint. It will enable you to simplify an otherwise overwhelming undertaking. It makes the journey of running a successful side hustle a lot easier. Last but not least, one reason why laying out a plan to start or scale your side hustle is important is because it helps to keep you committed. It is easy to give up when your passion isn't carrying you anymore, but looking at your plan will help to see the purpose behind your passion. Your plan and purpose will be the "WHY" to keep you going on the days when your passion doesn't carry you. It will help to keep you committed, focused, and consistent with your business goals. And seeing your plan written out is always a great way to see what you need to keep, adjust, and remove along your journey to success.

CHAPTER 4

Building Your Brand and Marketing Your Business

Your potential customers need to know you, like you, and trust you. Then they'll buy from you.

DEVELOPING THE LOOK AND FEEL OF YOUR BRAND

Branding is an incredibly important part of a business. It is essentially the look and feel of your business, and it ties directly into the way your potential customers perceive your business. This perception includes what they think about your online presence, your storefront, and the actual products and services you have to offer. And this perception is also important for building likeability and trust.

Branding is much more than just having a nice logo. So many people assume that once you have a nice logo, your branding is set, but a logo is just a small part of your overall brand. With so many businesses, products, and services competing for your potential customers' attention, your brand can be your key differentiator among your competition.

Developing the look and feel for your brand means creating a brand identity that ties into your business vision and mission, which we discussed earlier. Your brand identity is essentially made up of various components and design elements that create the image of your business for your customer. It includes your business name, logo, color palette, and typography/fonts. These pieces can then be leveraged to convey your brand identity through your website, storefront, social media presence, product packaging, customer emails, business cards, and more.

An example of a popular company with a great brand identity is Apple. Its brand identity is clean, sleek, and modern. Simple fonts, simple palettes, and a simple yet unmistakable logo. All of these elements encourage Apple's customers to focus on the technology and the quality of its products. You don't necessarily need to see the logo to know its product. In addition, this brand identity very much ties into its mission statement of "bringing the best user experience to its customers through its innovative hardware, software, and services."

When you have a strong brand identity, people easily recognize your business and know what to expect from you (quality and a great experience), and it becomes easier to reach and connect with your target audience. Plus, a strong brand identity can help validate your pricing so you are not perpetually selling at a discount—which is what happens to so many businesses that are overwhelmed by their competition but don't have a strong differentiator to carry them through.

So, let's get into some of the key pieces you need to craft a compelling look and feel for your brand.

The Name of Your Business

Your business name is likely to be one of the very first things people will remember about your business. And so, when it comes to naming your business, you want to make sure it's easy to remember, easy to pronounce, and easy to spell. Essentially, if I went to search for your business name on Instagram or Google, it should be a no-brainer for me without the additional exercise of trying to figure out how it's spelled, if it has multiple underscores or periods between letters, or any other likely confusing nuances. Simplicity is key, because the harder it is for people to find you, the more likely they are to give up and move on to the next business—and you don't want that!

To help you pick the right business name, my friend, Wonuola Okoye, a retail entrepreneur, business consultant, author of the *Startup Star*, and founder of Big Startup (www.bigstartup. co), has the following tips:

- **Leverage keywords.** Write down words relating to and describing your business, your brand, and other words you want to be incorporated. Get creative! The more keywords you can come up with, the more name combinations will be available. You can expand on your keyword list by adding synonyms.

- **Leverage tools to combine your keywords into potential names.** Free online name generator websites like Shopify's business name generator (shopify.com/tools), Word Lab (wordlab.com/name-generators), and Bust a Name (bustaname.com) can all help you come up with possible iterations of your potential business name as well as help check the domain availability.

- **Narrow down your options.** Once you have a good number of name options, the next step is to narrow things down. Try getting down to 10, then 5, then to your final 2. To help with this step, you can ask friends, family, and even potential customers what sounds best to them.

Your Business Logo

I mentioned earlier that your business logo isn't your *entire* brand identity, but it is the face of your business and will be your brand identifier on everything from your website to your social platforms to your marketing materials to your product packaging. As a result, you want to create a logo that is beautiful, stands out, and is easily recognizable.

There are so many incredible free online tools and resources to help you create a stunning logo. Websites like canva.com, wix.com, shopify.com, and more all offer logo design options. You can also hire a graphic designer on platforms like etsy.com, upwork.com, or fiverr.com to help you come up with some logo options. Keep in mind that as your business grows and evolves, so can your logo. So many brands have updated their logos over time to better reflect their brand identity. Even Clever Girl Finance has gone through logo (and brand) evolutions!

Regardless of whether you choose to design your logo yourself or to hire someone to design it for you, here's some additional advice from my friend Wonuola:

- **Create a tagline.** Write a few words that capture what your brand is before you start designing your logo. While not mandatory, your logo can be a visual translation or representation of those words. Alternatively, you can use your tagline alongside whatever logo you eventually decide on. *Hint: You can leverage your mission statement to pull a few words for this.*

■ **Make your logo inspiring, but don't overdesign it.** Pick something that's minimal but detailed enough to inspire all the other graphic elements you'll end up using to create your brand identity. It doesn't need to be complex, so don't worry about creating some big, extensive conceptual thing.

■ **Understand the difference between a logotype and a logomark.** A logotype is essentially the name of a business consisting of letters that are designed using unique typography. A logomark (or what most people refer to as a logo) is an identifying mark or symbol that does not contain the company name but stands for it. A logo by itself can't stand alone in terms of brand recognition, at least not until your brand becomes super-popular. Case in point: Apple, Nike, and Mercedes Benz all have incredibly strong brand recognition and you don't need to see their logotype to know it's their brand. However, in the early days of your business, it's great to have a logotype to always reinforce your brand name.

Now let's get into colors and fonts!

Colors and Fonts

You can consider your brand colors and fonts as the building blocks of your brand identity. Let's discuss each one.

■ **Brand colors.** Color is a great way to convey your brand identity, especially because colors can have different meanings and effects on your ideal customer. This meaning and effect can impact whether or not a person will be attracted to your business offerings, which is why it's a good idea to understand the basics of color psychology as you select a color palette for your business. Color psychology is basically how colors impact psychology, behavior, and emotions. Here are some color insights I've gleaned from research at colorpsychology.org:[1]

- *Red:* Associated with energy, danger, strength, power, and determination, as well as passion, desire, and love. It's known to stimulate appetite, so many food companies leverage this color. Colors related to red are magenta, burgundy, and maroon.

- *Yellow:* Associated with playfulness, joy, happiness, intellect, and energy. It produces a warming effect, arouses cheerfulness, and stimulates mental activity. It is also attention-grabbing (think traditional taxi cabs or the McDonald's sign). Yellow also indicates honor and loyalty. Colors related to yellow are amber and beige.

- *Green:* The color of nature that symbolizes growth, harmony, freshness, stability, and endurance. It has a strong emotional tie with safety. Darker greens are commonly associated with money and wealth. It is also commonly used to promote eco-friendliness as well as health and wellness.

- *Blue:* Comes across as enthusiastic, trustworthy, secure, and dependable. It can also represent being warm, communicative, and compassionate, as well as pure and clean. This is a common color in the banking and financial services space where trust is a big focal point. It is also commonly used with products representing cleanliness, like water and cleaning products. Colors related to blue are teal and turquoise.

- *Brown:* Associated with the traits of depth, richness, dependability, reliability, and resilience. Light brown represents honesty and stability, while dark brown is

---

[1]https://www.colorpsychology.org/

considered mature and predictable. It is commonly used to promote men's products.

- *Orange:* Combines the energy of red and the happiness of yellow. Associated with joy, sunshine, and the tropics. It represents enthusiasm, fascination, happiness, creativity, determination, attraction, success, encouragement, and stimulation. This color is also an appetite stimulator.

- *Pink:* Represents love, tenderness, and youth. It is a calming color. It is linked to hope and optimism. It also represents positive aspects of traditional femininity. It is commonly used to promote youthful products or female-specific products. A related color is salmon (a kind of light orangey pink).

- *Purple*: Combines the stability of blue and the energy of red and is associated with royalty. It symbolizes power, nobility, luxury, and ambition. It also conveys wealth and extravagance. Colors related to purple are indigo, violet, lavender, and mauve.

- *White*: Associated with light, goodness, and purity. Considered to be the color of perfection. It can also represent a successful beginning.

- *Black*: Associated with power, authority, elegance, formality, and mystery. It denotes strength and authority and is considered to be a very prestigious color.

  For more specifics on the color psychology of each of these colors and more, definitely visit the website colorpsychology.org. As you choose a color theme for your brand, you can leverage a combination of shades, tones, and accents to mix things up. Be mindful of overusing any one single color, as this can be overwhelming. Pinterest is great for pulling together color inspiration as you work on crafting your brand identity.

- **Brand fonts.** The fonts you use to convey your brand messaging are also known as your brand typography. As a general rule of thumb, you want your fonts to be easy on the eye and approachable. The last thing you want is for someone to click off from your website because the fonts were too small, too close together, or just generally hard to read. Some great font types to use when you have a lot of text are serif and sans serif fonts. A quick Google search will yield several varieties and options, but common examples include:

- *Serif fonts:* Times New Roman, Garamond, Baskerville, Georgia, Courier New.
- *Sans serif fonts:* Arial, Helvetica, Proxima Nova, Futura, and Calibri.

You may also choose to use one of the less common fonts you find via your search as well. Keep in mind that script fonts are typically harder to read when there's a lot of text, so it's a good idea to save them for accents and headers.

It's important to choose font combinations that you love and that speak to your style and brand identity. Your fonts will say a lot about your brand, so choose wisely.

Putting It All Together

Instead of just choosing all these components individually, you'll want to put all the pieces together to ensure you have a cohesive look and feel for your brand. You can tweak and adjust things as necessary until you feel your brand identity is being appropriately conveyed. As you work through this process, turn to tools like Pinterest and your everyday life to find inspiration for the look and feel of your brand.

One incredibly helpful resource you can create is a brand guide. Your brand guide essentially helps to communicate how the pieces that make up your brand identity should be used. This resource can be an important reminder as your business grows and can act as a guideline for any employees or contractors you hire to support your business, so they know how to maintain your brand consistency. This guide should include an overview of your brand, how your logo should be used, your brand color codes, fonts and font sizes, and other guidance on how your brand should and should not be represented.

Take Action

Now it's time to work on the look and feel of your brand! Use the suggestions in this section to choose or fine-tune the following:

- **Your business name.** If you need help coming up with ideas, take advantage of the various free online name generator websites like Shopify's business name generator (shopify.com/tools), Word Lab (wordlab.com/name-generators), and Bust a Name (bustaname.com).
- **Your business logo.** You can take a stab at designing your own via websites like canva.com, wix.com, and shopify .com or you can hire a graphic designer on platforms like etsy.com, upwork.com, or fiverr.com.
- **Your colors and fonts.** Considering the principles of color psychology, pick the colors you feel will work best for your brand. Also research simple, easy-to-read fonts that you can tie into your overall brand identity. Spend some time on Pinterest creating boards to help inspire the process.
- **Establish a brand guide.** This document will help communicate how the various pieces of your brand identity should be used to ensure consistency throughout your brand.

CREATING A MARKETABLE BRAND STORY

Stories are extremely powerful—they're a major way humans forge connections and relate to one another. Your brand story is essentially the narrative of your business that can help you connect with your ideal customers. It showcases how and why you started your business, and what your purpose is. It is an essential add-on to your website's "about" page—the same place featuring your business vision and mission statement. It can also be woven throughout your content and marketing strategy (which we'll get into in the next section) to drive customer engagement.

A compelling brand story makes you memorable, establishes trust, and ties into your customers' overall experience with your business by allowing you to create an emotional connection and bond with them that goes beyond a mere financial transaction.

In this day and age, customers want to connect with brands on a deeper level than just fancy packaging. They want to connect with brands that not only solve their problems and meet their needs but also align with their values and make them feel prioritized. If done right, your brand story can create loyal customers and raving fans, which in turn will directly impact the growth of your business.

Take Clever Girl Finance, for instance. Our brand story, which is one of our top-visited website pages (clevergirlfinance .com/about-bola), is all about my mother's personal experiences navigating her finances as a young woman and my similar experiences trying to figure out finances on my own, given the lack of relevant resources. It leans into the importance of financial wellness for women and highlights our mission of empowering women with the right tools and resources to achieve that financial wellness. I drew upon my personal story and experiences to create a relatable and compelling brand story to attract the women our brand wants to reach: women who are figuring out their finances and want to achieve financial wellness in a relatable, fun, nonjudgmental, and nonshaming way.

Having a brand story is not just important for building lasting relationships with your customers; it's also important for anyone who works with you, whether they are partners, contractors, or employees. Your story impacts the culture and operations of your business and helps anyone who works with you to understand your business purpose and the potential impact they can make in your business and the lives of your customers. It can also serve as a form of motivation for you, as you run and grow your business.

That being said, let's talk about how to craft your own compelling brand story.

How to Craft Your Brand Story

As you start to think about your brand story, reflect on the experiences that brought you to this point. You'll want to craft an authentic narrative that represents you and your business. Here are some key tips:

- **Start with your mission statement.** Earlier, we discussed creating a mission statement, and this is a great foundation to build your brand story on. Since your mission statement highlights your business objectives, who your business is for, and how it positively impacts your customers and/or your community, you can use it to identify the values you want your brand story to convey.

- **Take a deep dive into the details of why you started your business.** This is where you can really tell the story of your brand without having to stick to one or two sentences. Write down how you had the initial flash of inspiration to start your business, what compelled you to start it, and what you were experiencing. Talk about how you've gotten to where you are today and why you believe in what your business offers. Include any interesting facts that can help establish a bond with your customers.

- **Know your audience.** As you craft your brand story, remember that you are not writing it for yourself. You are writing it for that ideal customer you want to attract. Think about your customer avatars you built earlier, and write as if you're speaking to that person to develop the tone and style for your story. It's usually a good idea to showcase your personality, passion, and even humor in your brand story so it doesn't feel generic or cookie-cutter. This will help your business stand out and make your brand more relatable.

Take Action

Grab your piece of paper or notebook and jot down the first draft of your brand story with help from the tips in this section.

- Start with your mission statement and build your story from there. Include your business vision and values.
- Lean into the details of why you started your business. Don't be shy. This is your opportunity to really express your *why* and the meaningfulness of what you do.
- Create a story that speaks to and engages your ideal customers. They will be the ones reading it. You want to pull them in and really connect with them in your narrative.

As with other parts of your business, your brand story will evolve and change as your business grows.

YOUR ONLINE PRESENCE AND CONTENT STRATEGY

In today's world, it's almost impossible to have a business without having some sort of online presence, be it your own website or social media accounts on one or more platforms. It's now second nature for people to do a quick Google or Instagram hashtag search to learn more about a business, read reviews, or find contact information. In addition to having an online presence, creating consistent and relevant content is more important than ever in order to stay top-of-mind with your ideal customers. Given the fast pace of social media, you want to stand out among the many distractions competing for their attention. When it comes time for your ideal customer to purchase a product or service that you offer, you want them to think of you first, and consistent content creation can help to make that happen. It reminds them of your business's name and what you do, along with a touch of personality.

Having an online presence is a foundational aspect for any business because it can be such an incredible marketing tool. In my opinion, creating your own website should be your first step to establishing your online presence, because this is essentially your home base and a platform you own. You pay for your domain name, you pay for your website hosting, you own it.

When you really think about it (and you read the crazy fine-print agreements that we knowingly or unknowingly agree to. . .*yikes*), you may have a presence and build a following on the many social platforms that exist today, but neither the platform nor the following you build actually belongs to you; they belong to the platform in question. This means if Instagram or Facebook shut down today, your presence on those platforms and the audience you've built there would go away, and you have no control over that. If these platforms decide to make changes to their algorithms, limiting who can see your updates (which they do all the time. . .*argh!*), there's also absolutely nothing you can do about it.

With your website, on the other hand, unless you intentionally shut it down, or your domain or hosting subscription lapses, you have complete control over your site and the content you share there.

For example, with Clever Girl Finance, today we have a following of hundreds of thousands of amazing people across multiple social media platforms. And while we constantly create content on those social platforms and stay engaged with our audience, we do recognize that we don't own any of that. That makes our website extremely important, and we intentionally direct our social media audiences to our website so they know where to find us even if we lose access to a social platform.

On our website, we share all the details about our business, publish new articles on the site every day, and offer our completely free courses and additional free resources there. We share teasers of our content throughout social media, but we always direct people back to our website (our home base) for the full content. Constantly keeping our site updated and on topic also helps us to rank higher on Google search. This ranking allows us to attract a whole new audience that might not already be aware of our presence on the various social platforms.

I don't know about you, but if I'm trying to find a business, while I might sometimes do an Instagram handle search, one of the first things I do is exit whatever social media platform I'm on and head straight to Google to do a search about the business, find their contact information, read online reviews, and see who their competition is. You probably do the same thing. And if you and I behave in this way, then it's more than likely your ideal customers are doing the same thing too!

Because customers are going to be searching for you this way, I can't stress enough the importance of having your own online home base. Time and time again, I see business owners who are based solely on social media and don't have a website. Their businesses (and thereby their revenue) are directly impacted by the constant algorithm changes the various social platforms make. Even if they have a large following on these platforms, new algorithms can mean each post is reaching a smaller and smaller audience unless the business is paying for ads—because those social platforms are looking to make money, too.

As a result of not having a website, these businesses are missing out on the opportunity to attract new audiences via Google and other search engines. Also, no matter what type of business you have, having a website is a way of establishing credibility. There are many times I've found a company on Instagram, searched for their website, found nothing, and because of this, did not make a purchase.

In addition to the points I've just made, when you have your own website, you can also better showcase your products and services, provide clear access to customer service (this is a big one—ever seen the angry comments people leave on social media when they don't have access to the customer service contact for a business?!), and share updates and content that might be too lengthy or detailed for the fast pace of social media.

With all of that being said, let's get into how you can establish (or improve) your online presence and create a content strategy to engage with your ideal customers and stay top-of-mind when it's time to buy.

Establishing Your Online Presence

As mentioned earlier, when it comes to establishing your online presence, it's a good idea to start out by creating a dedicated website for your business.

To do this, you'll need to register for a domain name and a website host. Sites like squarespace.com and wix.com are great for getting domain names, website hosting, and website templates all in one place. These can be great options, especially if you are working on a budget and looking for an easy site builder so you can create your own website—without having to hire a website developer right away.

If you already have a website design, sites like godaddy.com and bluehost.com are highly rated when it comes to domain names and website hosting. Each of these sites will guide you step-by-step on what you need to do on their platforms to set up your website (or transfer an existing site).

While there are many different pages and types of content you can feature on your website, you want to make sure it at least includes these core pages:

- **Homepage.** Your homepage is typically the first point of entry for many customers who visit your website, so you want to make sure you are putting your best foot forward.

It should be visually pleasing, easy to navigate, and have clearly visible links to all your other core pages. On your homepage, you want to share a brief overview of your business, showcase your best products and services, and share a couple of your favorite testimonials or reviews. You can even highlight a snippet of your brand story.

- **About page.** Your about page is likely to be another one of your most-visited pages. If a customer has never done business with you before, they will visit this page to learn more about who is behind the business as a way to establish credibility and a level of comfort before they make a purchase. The about page is a great opportunity to share more about who you are, your company mission and values, and your brand story, as we went over earlier.

- **Products and/or services page(s).** Here's your chance to make your products or services really shine. This is the perfect location to feature photos of your products (or your service in action), detailed descriptions, the benefits of each product or service, how they are different than your competition, and why your ideal customer should buy from you. If you have multiple products or services, you can also categorize them accordingly on this page and link out to their subcategory pages if needed, making all the information easy to find.

- **FAQ page.** Having a page dedicated to your frequently asked questions (FAQs) is a great idea. Not only will having this page save you a ton of time (since you won't have to repeat these answers over and over again), but each answer you provide is also an opportunity to convince a potential customer to purchase from you by eliminating any doubts they might have. It's certainly worth the time to create this page. You can start by brainstorming questions yourself, and adding any new ones as your customers actually start asking them.

- **Testimonials page.** Great and authentic testimonials can be an excellent credibility and sales tool for your business. The best testimonials will highlight a customer's experience of how your product and/or service positively impacted them. Showcasing real people (with photos, names, social media profiles, etc.) can really help to drive home the impact and authenticity of your testimonials and inspire your ideal customer to make a purchase.

- **Blog.** Having a blog is something that is essential to any business (in my opinion). Your blog is a great place to create content on a variety of topics relevant to your business, thus allowing you to showcase your expertise and passion for your field. If executed properly, your blog can be your most effective marketing tool, as it can drive traffic to your site, establish credibility, and in turn convert your blog readers into valuable leads and sales.

- **Press and updates page.** If you've been featured by any media, this is a great place to share those accomplishments. For instance, you can include links to articles, videos, podcasts, or social posts that have mentioned your business. This page acts as another way to establish trust and build credibility with your ideal customers.

- **Contact and customer service page.** It's important to have an easy-to-find page providing the information customers need to get in contact with you to ask questions or report issues. It also makes it easy for people to reach out to you for media and collaboration opportunities. Be sure to include an email address (or a form that goes to a frequently checked email address), your social media handles if applicable, and a phone number (if you choose).

- **Privacy policy, terms and conditions, and disclosures pages.** In today's world where privacy is constantly being invaded, terms and conditions are often unclear, and disclosures are not being disclosed (no pun intended), you want to be transparent and put your customers' minds at ease. Differentiate yourself from the competition by letting visitors to your site know how any personal information and data they provide will be used, the terms and conditions they'll need to agree to if they choose to browse your site or make a purchase, and any other pertinent information they should be aware of. Ideally, these can be set up as individual pages accessible from the footer section of your website. There are also many legal sites like nolo.com and legalzoom.com that provide templates for these pages that you can customize specifically to your location and business.

Now that you have a baseline of what to include on your website, let's talk about creating consistent content.

Creating a Content Strategy

The whole idea behind consistent content creation is to keep your ideal customer continuously engaged with relevant and valuable content until they are ready to make a purchase from you (and afterward, too). Doing this essentially makes sure they don't forget what your business has to offer among all the other distractions in their lives.

However, staying top-of-mind for your ideal customer requires having more than a website. It requires creating content not just on your website (e.g., blog posts) but on the social platforms (e.g., Instagram, Facebook, Pinterest, Twitter, etc.) that your ideal customer frequents.

Because there are several different popular social platforms, it's easy to get overwhelmed trying to share your business and stay on top of all of them. To avoid the overwhelm, it's a good idea to start with one platform, and then add on others once you get into a content creation flow.

For instance, with Clever Girl Finance, we create a ton of content on multiple platforms today, but it hasn't always been that way. Going back to when it was a team of me, myself, and yours truly, I started creating content first on the blog. Once I got the hang of things there, I moved on to Instagram, and then on to YouTube, and as the team grew, we added several other platforms. What allowed me to do this successfully was leveraging the power of planning: laying out a content strategy and creating a content schedule, which is also essentially the first step to creating a marketing plan.

Your content strategy. Establishing a content strategy is an integral part of marketing your business. It specifically refers to how you'll lay out, distribute, and manage the different pieces of content you create for your business. Your content allows your ideal customer to get to know you and your brand, showcases your expertise in your industry, and educates potential customers.

Content comes in a variety of forms, be it written content (blog posts and social media captions), visual content (Instagram and Pinterest posts), video content (YouTube, IGTV), or audio content (podcasts). What you decide to create really depends on what's easiest to get started with and what resonates with your target audience (which you'll fine-tune over time based on how people respond). As you consider what form of content to create, you want to take into consideration the following:

- Who is consuming your content (keep your customer avatars in mind)
- The problem you are solving for your ideal customers
- Your unique perspectives and angles for the content you'll create
- The forms of content you will create, e.g., blog posts, photos or infographics, podcast episodes, videos, etc.
- The channels you will use to showcase or share your content

You'll need to spend some time brainstorming different content ideas and doing research for each piece of content you create to make sure it will resonate with your audience and they'll be able to find it if they search with hashtags, keywords, etc. It's not a bad idea to see what kind of content your competition is creating (or not creating).

A key topic to read up on and learn more about is Search Engine Optimization (SEO), which is essentially the process of improving your site to increase its visibility for relevant searches.[2] One of my favorite websites with a ton of free resources is moz .com (look up their beginner's guide to SEO). Some of my favorite books on SEO and content creation in general (that are totally worth reading) are *Content Inc.* by Joe Pulizzi and *Top of Mind* by John Hall.

Once your content strategy is in place—i.e., you've defined your core content ideas, what forms you'll create, and which platforms you'll use to share it—you'll need to create some form of content management process. Enter your content schedule.

Your content schedule. Your content schedule is the second part of your content strategy. It is basically an established plan of when and where you will be publishing the content you create. If you don't have a content schedule in place, you might find that you forget to create content, or don't do it as often as you could. Having a content schedule in place allows you to plan your content ahead of time and stay organized.

As a business owner, this is particularly important if you are juggling a full-time job or other life obligations like being a mom or caregiver. It also makes sure you have the opportunity to plan out and get ahead on content tied to specific holidays and other high-sales seasons that could potentially bring in extra revenue for your business. It shows you the big picture of what's coming up. Plus, if you find that you need to hire support as your business grows, your content schedule is essentially part of a transferable process you can delegate.

---

[2]https://searchengineland.com/guide/what-is-seo

Your content schedule can be divided into two parts for organization purposes—your editorial content and your promotional content. Your editorial content is the content you create to educate and inform your audience, show life behind the scenes at your business, tell a story, etc. Your promotional content is the content specifically tied to sales, offers, any seasonal campaigns you are running, and any content promoting your products and services.

Once you've laid out what kind of content you'll be publishing, the next step is to develop a calendar of specific dates to publish and share each piece of content on each of the platforms you've selected. To easily keep track of your upcoming planned content, you can build a simple Google Sheet or Excel spreadsheet with columns that highlight the specific details or link to the content, the platform where it will be published, the target publication date, its completion status, and a date to republish the content if applicable.

You can also leverage project management tools like Asana or Trello to create your calendar and keep track of the tasks involved. There are also tools like Later Media, HootSuite, SmarterQueue, and Buffer, which allow you to automate your scheduling process by setting them to post content on your chosen date and time (or notifying you to post).

At Clever Girl Finance, our content schedule is a well-oiled machine that we depend on to stay consistent with creating and sharing the content we produce. Without it, especially with the amount of content we create today, we'd be completely lost. We use a combination of tools to manage our content schedule: Asana to plan things out and assign dates, Later Media for Instagram scheduling, and SmarterQueue for Facebook, LinkedIn, and Pinterest scheduling.

Again, it's a good idea to start with just one platform (which is what I did), and only add more once you've gotten into the swing of things and have established your content creation and scheduling flow.

Now that you know how to create a content strategy and content schedule, it's time to get yours going!

Take Action

Leverage the suggestions in this section to create your own content strategy. Start by answering these questions:

- Who is consuming your content?
- What problem you are solving for your ideal customers that you can address in the content you create?
- What is your unique take and angle to add your own spin to the content you create?
- What forms of content will you create? E.g., blog posts, images, podcast episodes, videos, etc.
- Which channels will you use to showcase or share your content?

Once your content strategy is in place, take some time to lay out your content schedule:

- On a calendar, assign specific dates to publish and share each piece of content you create on each of the platforms you've selected. You can create a Google or Excel spreadsheet or use the calendar feature in a project management tool like Asana or Trello.
- Set reminders to frequently review and update your calendar. This way you can plan ahead for seasonal initiatives, holidays, and your personal schedule, while still creating informational content to keep your business top-of-mind for your ideal customer.

YOUR MARKETING STRATEGY AND LEVELING UP YOUR GAME

So, let's talk about marketing strategies! If you are serious about making sales and growing your business, you are going to need to establish some sort of marketing approach or strategy. This is essentially your plan to promote and sell your products or services in order to generate revenue and profits. And while having a website and content strategy in place is foundational to creating a marketing strategy, there are many additional ways to market your business so you can meet your sales and growth goals.

When it comes to marketing your products or services, your primary focus should be threefold: delivering value to your potential customers, sharing the benefits your products or services provide (and the pain points they solve), and convincing your potential customers of why they should buy specifically from *you* by showcasing your industry expertise and the things that make you stand out.

Your marketing strategy should include all of this—not just a direct call to buy, buy, buy. Constant direct calls to purchase without adding any value, education, or insight typically don't resonate with potential customers. You need to provide an opportunity for them to get to know you, like you, and trust you before you ask for their money!

Executing your marketing strategy starts by combining what you know about your ideal customer, the problem they need to be solved, and what your competition is currently doing (their strengths, weaknesses, and potential opportunities). You'll use all this information to come up with a series of plans that will uniquely position you in front of that ideal customer with the goal of making sales.

Setting Your Marketing Goals

A successful strategy starts with you outlining specific and measurable marketing and sales goals you want to achieve and setting a timeline to accomplish them. Having goals in place gives you a "north star" to help track the progress of your strategy and adjust it as needed based on the results you get. Your marketing goals could revolve around promoting new products or services, establishing your brand, targeting new customers, upselling to existing customers, increasing your sales, or maximizing your profits. (After all, the whole point of marketing boils down to getting customers and making money!)

Once you've laid out your marketing goals, the next step is to determine what specific marketing strategies you can test out and implement to help you achieve those goals.

Marketing Strategies to Achieve Your Goals

There are a variety of marketing strategies that, if executed the right way, can help your business grow, get you in front of new customers, and increase your sales and profits. While there is no guarantee that a marketing strategy will work, it's worth testing out a few to determine what methods are most successful and then make tweaks and adjustments to improve their outcomes. Let's get into some of the popular marketing strategies to help you level up your business game.

Social media marketing. I mentioned this earlier as part of creating your content strategy (which also ties into marketing), but it's worth mentioning again because social media marketing is incredibly important in today's world where people own multiple devices and are constantly online. This means there are so many platforms and opportunities to catch and keep your ideal client's attention and reach audiences that you otherwise would not be able to. Popular social media content platforms at the time of this writing are Facebook, Instagram, YouTube, TikTok, and Pinterest.

Email marketing. Unlike social media marketing, email marketing is all about building an email list of potential customers that you can communicate with and promote to at any given time. Your email marketing initiatives are not impacted by algorithms, because this is a list you own, so this can be a great way to promote your expertise and your business.

With email marketing, it's important that you don't overwhelm your subscribers with too many emails too quickly. You do, however, want to be consistent with your emails to stay top-of-mind with your audience, but limit yourself to sending them once a week or biweekly so people don't get annoyed and unsubscribe. You should also only email people who have opted into your email list. Adding people to your list who did not opt in can negatively impact your brand image and make it more likely for your emails to be marked as spam. You also don't want to buy email lists for these same reasons. At the end of the day, you want to build an email list that is engaged, wants to hear from you, values your business, and loves your brand.

Paid advertising. This is essentially paying for promotional product or service content placement, either online or in traditional media (radio, television, etc.). Today, it's more common (and cost-effective) for people to leverage social media for their paid advertising strategy. Facebook ads, Instagram ads, YouTube ads, Pinterest ads, etc. are all relatively easy to set up, and your ad spend can be customized specifically for your budget.

Each of these platforms now has step-by-step tutorials on how to set up ads, and there are plenty of free resources online that can guide you through it and provide extra tips for success. If you choose to do paid marketing, it's worth spending the time to learn how it works and how to set it up yourself (unless you have a massive budget and want to hire someone to manage it for you).

With paid advertising, you'll want to lean on your customer avatar to determine the audiences you want to target, and then run a series of variations (ad tests) to help you determine what ad type is resonating best (and at the lowest cost) with your target audience.

Collaborations. Another great way to market your business (and one that has really helped Clever Girl Finance grow) is collaborations. This could mean partnering with businesses in parallel spaces or partnering with bigger or smaller brands to cross-promote your brands to each other's audiences. The great thing about collaborations is that there are so many ways to do it. You could do joint brand giveaways, content exchange series, guest posts on one another's blogs, a joint online or in-person event—the opportunities are endless.

Events. Online and in-person events are another great marketing strategy. Not only do you get to market your brand and your products or services, but you also have the opportunity to network directly with your ideal customers. This is an incredible way for them to learn more about you and vice versa. Talking to your customers lets you gain valuable insights about who they are and what they want, which in turn can help you fine-tune your customer avatars, improve your products and services, and adjust your marketing strategy.

Giveaways. Running giveaways of your products and services can help to grow your audience by exposing new people to your brand for the first time. However, it's important to clearly outline your goals for the giveaway, because they may attract people who are just looking for free stuff and won't necessarily become loyal brand followers. As a result, some of this audience can quickly dissipate once the giveaway has concluded. Examples of giveaway goals could be creating product or service awareness, leveraging a free product or service to promote a priced product or service, or simply growing your audience. You also want to make sure that any giveaways you choose to run aren't going to cost you too much. You can reduce costs by running a contest-style giveaway, where unlimited people can enter and just a few will win your prizes. This is also a potential way to get more email list subscribers.

Word of mouth. This marketing strategy is by far the most effective because it's all about people telling their friends and family about your products and services. The reason it works so well is that people are more likely to buy from a business if they get a personal recommendation, especially if they are not yet familiar with the business. They know they can trust the word of their relative or friend, and that goes a lot further than even the best advertisement could. I definitely value personal recommendations and make a lot of my purchases that way if it's not a mainstream or popular brand that I already know. People also ask their personal circle whether anyone has heard of a certain brand before they make a first purchase, so word of mouth can be beneficial in this scenario as well.

Establishing word of mouth, specifically positive word of mouth, comes from a combination of different things, including a visually appealing online presence, great products and services, valuable and informational content, and exceptional customer service. Essentially, every step you take to make your business amazing will also boost the reputation of your business and naturally encourage word of mouth. If there's one thing people do well, it's talk, and talk can spread like wildfire!

If you'd like to sweeten the deal a little bit, you can start a referral program for your business. Reward the new customer and the person who referred them by offering them a coupon, free product voucher, etc. This gives people extra incentive to recommend you!

These are just a few marketing strategies that you can start to test out, fine-tune, and leverage to grow your business. Start with one and go from there! The perfect market strategy is the one that works effectively—not just to attract your ideal customer but to motivate them to make a purchase from you!

Take Action

On a piece of paper or in a notebook:

- Outline some specific marketing goals that you'd like to pursue for your side hustle. Whether it's growing your audience, creating brand awareness, or increasing sales, defining your goals first is foundational to your marketing strategy.

- Next, select a marketing strategy to begin implementing and build a timeline for how long you want to test this strategy.

- Schedule time once a week, biweekly, or at the very least monthly to review the results, and to make tweaks and adjustments to your strategy as necessary.

- Add on additional strategies to test out. Rinse and repeat the test cycle and take notes on what marketing methods are proving most successful.

MEET KALYN JOHNSON CHANDLER

Kalyn is the founder and creative director of Effie's Paper :: Stationery&Whatnot (effiespaper.com), a lifestyle brand catering to women, particularly women who are often overlooked by other lifestyle brands. Effie's Paper products are sold on six different online platforms and in over 200+ independent retailers across the United States, Canada, and Haiti. It is also a certified MWBE (Minority Owned Women Business Enterprise). Kalyn is a graduate of the prestigious Goldman Sachs 10,000 Small Businesses Program and was one of a handful of Instagram influencers to be singled out by *The Washington Post* as a brand/influencer with authentic messaging during the COVID-19 pandemic.

Effie's Paper :: Stationery & Whatnot has a beautiful and unmistakable brand. How did you come up with the look for your brand and what was your inspiration?
The look and feel of the brand have evolved over time. Since the company is named after my maternal grandmother, Mrs. Effie Hayes, our name definitely has an old-timey feel to it. Despite this fact, I wanted our branding to feel modern and hip to reflect the fact that while named after my grandmother, we are a modern lifestyle brand. Our color palette has changed too. We're

currently in our third evolution and decided to go with hot pink and white because of the way hot pink pops off the page as well as on computer and phone screens. I wanted the look and the feel of the brand to be colorful and bright, but hip.

The inspiration behind our overall look and feel is our customer. She's fun, energetic, smart, motivated, and yes, she loves pretty things! I wanted our branding to reflect these characteristics. In addition, I wanted our logo, company colors, and products to be easily recognizable and appealing to our target audience. The use of modern fonts, bright colors, and clean design are the underlying tenets of the brand's look and feel.

Can you share a bit about your brand story and how you came up with it?

Believe it or not, Effie's Paper :: Stationery&Whatnot started out as a personalized stationery company. I started Effie's Paper because I wasn't finding stationery products that made my heart leap. My grandmother fostered my love of all things paper, so it was natural to name the company after her. Including "whatnot" in the name was intentional—I figured I'd want to add "whatnots" in at some point. That some point turned out to be a lot sooner rather than later with the onslaught of digital communication. When text messaging and emails began to supplant the art of letter writing, I phased out personalized correspondence and introduced our "whatnots" to stay relevant. This pivot resulted in the iteration of the brand you see currently. Today, we are a lifestyle brand presenting cool and on-trend accessories for fun at work, stylish travel, and a chic daily life. The goal was simple: to create lifestyle products that could coexist with today's technology. *Et voilà!* We offer our online customers and wholesale accounts an on-trend, curated selection of stylish desk, stationery, and travel and gift accessories. Our products motivate, inspire, foster female empowerment, and are a unique mix of casual elegance, motivation, and social conversation that makes using them fun and engaging.

Our credo is: "The future is female and is being shaped by the power of Black Girl Magic!" We believe that from the door to her desk, a woman should be surrounded by pretty things that make her heart leap! Outwardly, we're all about pretty, but Effie's Paper is pretty with a purpose. At our core, we are about female empowerment, promoting equity for women of color, and advocating for women and girls. I've always been a "girl's girl" if you will; I believe in women supporting women and wanted my brand to be reflective of this belief. When I introduced "whatnots" into our product catalog, I began to think about phrases and slogans that would promote our brand values and resonate with our audience. In addition, although I was late to the social media party, I knew that social media would play a large role in our marketing efforts. And since social media has a tendency to amplify everything, I saw this as an opportunity to help build a community centered around shared beliefs and experiences.

Your personality is tied into your brand as well; why did you choose to incorporate yourself into your branding strategy?
Ironically, it was never my intention to become the face of the brand. To be perfectly honest, I had absolutely no interest in being personally associated with the brand. I had this unrealistic notion that having a website on the internet meant that I could be invisible. However, sharing our company values was a no-brainer for me; our values are my values and I'm a firm believer in standing up for what I believe in. But the idea of posting my photo on our website, on social media, and in our marketing materials made me cringe. I felt like I was too brown and not young enough. At the time, though, I had a social media manager who pushed me to step out of my comfort zone. And, bit by bit, I did. I had no intention of becoming the face of the brand, but God bless her for having the foresight to see what I could not. She was right—people are curious about the person behind the brand. And ultimately, people buy from other people. So, while it wasn't my

intention to be upfront and center, I am. This has its good and not-so-good points. At first blush, it's pretty obvious that Effie's Paper is a Black-female-owned business with a mission to empower women. Has being the face of the brand and sharing my personal values and opinions had a negative effect? I think it goes without saying that these two facts make it clear that Effie's Paper isn't going to appeal to everyone. But my identity and perspective as a Black woman are my superpowers. When I stopped trying to fit in with the majority, the brand began to flourish.

How has your branding evolved over time?
Over the course of time, everything about the brand has become much more polished and professional. I created our very first logo in a Word document. My childhood best friend became a self-taught web developer and made our first website, and the list goes on. There was so much that I didn't know at the beginning, but I knew that I needed to create an enticing online presence. Today we're light-years from where we were, but I've accepted that perfection doesn't exist! However, there are many ways to hone and refine different elements of your brand. Professional photography, skilled web developers, talented copywriters, graphic designers, and the like. Over time I've learned that making an investment in our branding directly correlates to our bottom line.

Why is branding so important for a business owner, even if their business is only a side hustle?
Today, with the proliferation of small businesses, it's more important than ever to have a cohesive brand story to stand out from the competition. First impressions are lasting ones. Once you've solidified your product or service, investing time and money to develop your brand is key, however big or small your business is. Branding determines how people perceive your company and can drive new business and sales. In essence, you want your branding to succinctly tell your customers what your company is about and who it's for at first blush. More and more, Instagram

is becoming a calling card for companies. People will check out a company's Instagram feed before going to their website. But it's important to realize that your brand story extends far beyond your website and social media feeds. To properly brand your business, your brand story should be interwoven into everything from your monthly newsletters to your invoices to your packaging. Attention to detail and thoughtfulness speak volumes about you and your brand.

What's the one branding tip you'd give someone building their business?

As you start building your business and brand story, it's crucial to know and understand your target audience. It's virtually impossible to craft a brand story if you don't know who you are selling to and what problem you are solving for her. Identifying your target audience at the outset will help you make decisions about tone/voice, colors, packaging, etc. Who you're selling to drives so much of your brand story that if you haven't pinned this down, it complicates things that should be relatively simple. I know on one hand that this sounds crazy, of course you know who you're selling to, right? BUT, do you really? Have you taken the time to map out her likes and dislikes? Do you know what Instagram accounts she follows and why? Who's her favorite musician? Where does she shop? The answers to these sorts of questions are vitally important to helping you craft your brand story, yet they are questions that many entrepreneurs fail to ask themselves. It's worth it to take the time to get clear on who you're selling to so that your time and money spent crafting your brand and running your business are well-spent.

CHAPTER 5

Business Finances—Let's Talk Money!

Staying on top of your business finances is not just to generate revenue; it's to make sure your profits stay in your pocket!

LAYING OUT YOUR STARTUP COSTS AND OPERATING EXPENSES

Let's talk money! If you've been part of the Clever Girl Finance community for a while or have read my first two books (*Clever Girl Finance: Ditch Debt, Save Money, and Build Real Wealth* and *Clever Girl: Learn How Investing Works, Grow Your Money*), you already know that money is one of my absolute favorite topics!

When you create a solid plan for your finances, then execute it and adjust it accordingly over time, you put yourself in a position where you are able to make your financial goals a reality. Achieving these goals creates options that enable you to live your life on your own terms.

Having multiple streams of income is essential to any financial plan, and as you know, one solid way to add an additional stream of income is by having a side hustle. However, if you don't have a proper plan in place for your business finances, then the money you earn will find ways to slip through your fingers (which is what money does best if you aren't telling it what to do!). If that happens, you'll find that you've spent all this time (long hours and no sleep) working a business, and for what? The last thing we want to do is work aimlessly and let our money slip away, #nothankyou. Plus, let's not forget the regret of wasted time—been there, done that, got the T-shirt #nothankyoutimestwo.

The state of your business finances can make or break your business, and it's not just about how much money you are making. You can have the most innovative business idea, a killer brand, and a business plan or marketing strategy that's totally on point, but if your business finances are not in order, your business will eventually crumble and fall apart. Having a solid financial foundation in place for your business should not be optional. It's something that you absolutely have to do if you want to succeed.

It all boils down to money and knowing how to properly manage the finances around your business. I see way too many people running side hustles who sidestep or overlook this all-too-important and very essential piece of the business success puzzle, but that's not going to be you, especially once you're done with this book!

Yes, you have your amazing business idea that is going to give you the opportunity to pursue your true passion and let you do what really love. This is the hustle that's going to get you out of the 9–5 and into your dream life, and you've seen it all play out in your head. You have been following the action steps in this book and you are ready to build your empire. But before you go off spending tons of money on branding, production, and marketing, let's take some time to break down what it's really going to cost you.

Estimating Your Startup Expenses

To establish a solid plan, we need to start at the very beginning by estimating your startup expenses, aka startup costs.

If your business is already up and running, you can skip ahead to the section right after this one that covers operating expenses. However, it could still be valuable for you to read this section, because knowing how much you spent setting up your business gives you the opportunity to reflect on those costs, review the foundations of your business finances, and gauge your progress over time.

Your startup expenses are the costs you incur to get your business up and running. They are different from your operating expenses, which are recurring expenses that you typically pay every month, quarter, or year.

For instance, a startup expense could be website design, because this is typically a one-time expense you'll have to pay—you won't be redesigning your website every single month. On the other hand, an operating expense could be website hosting—a fee you'll pay on a monthly basis to keep your website actively visible online.

Being intentional about your startup costs lets you create an initial spending plan to get your business up and running. It also acts as the beginning of your business budget. As your business becomes profitable, you'll be able to compare your baseline startup costs against your current revenue to judge how much financial progress you've made to keep you on track.

For example, I spent about $6,000 setting up Clever Girl Finance over several months when it first started as a side hustle (it took me about five months to officially launch the business). This amount included the initial branding, the website, and our very first line of planners. While I stuck to my initial spending plan, in retrospect, there were areas where I didn't need to spend so much and areas where the spending was totally worth it. Today, I use that $6,000 as the baseline when I'm measuring year-over-year growth, and we sure have come a long way!

As you think about your startup costs, here are my suggestions around what startup expenses a business owner should be considering. You can fill in the gaps as it relates to your own specific business:

- Domain name registration (e.g., www.xyz.com)
- Custom email accounts (e.g., info@xyz.com)
- Business registration fees (state and federal)
- Trademark fees (state and federal)
- Branding (logo and fonts)
- Website design
- Initial website hosting fees
- Initial advertising/marketing expenses
- Initial certifications or courses
- Equipment (computer, printer/scanner)
- Office supplies

- Product samples
- Initial product inventory

Once you have your necessary startup expenses all laid out, be sure to price out each item on your list. This way, you'll have a good idea of how much money you'll need to fund your business initially to get it off the ground, and you'll also have a baseline to measure against.

Operating Expenses

The next set of expenses you'll have are your operating costs. These are the expenses that are incurred on an ongoing basis to keep your business running. They are important to be aware of, because these are the expenses that will be coming your way most likely every single month, and you need to plan for them so you can pay for them.

Your operating expenses can be broken down into two categories: fixed operating expenses and variable operating expenses. Let's go over each type so you can plan for them accordingly.

- **Your fixed operating expenses.** These are expenses that typically do not change from month to month, regardless of your business sales or production changes. Some examples of fixed operating expenses include business insurance, internet services, tools subscriptions, website hosting fees, virtual assistant fees, rent, etc.

- **Your variable operating expenses.** These expenses vary from month to month because they are directly tied to your business activity—for instance, having higher or lower product manufacturing needs. Variable costs can include the raw materials for your products, inventory management, production costs, third-party payment processing tools, shipping fees, advertising fees, event expenses, etc.

If you have quarterly or annual operating expenses, you can divide them by 3 (for quarterly, since there are three months in each quarter) or 12 months (for annual expenses) to determine your true monthly expenses. As a very simplistic example, you might have one $100/month cost, one $600/quarter cost (divides to $200/month), and one $3600/year cost (divides to $300/month). In this example, your true monthly expenses are $600.

You also want to keep in mind that as your business grows or as you start offering new products and services, your variable operating expenses will most likely grow with these additions while your fixed expenses will remain the same. Once you've mapped out what your operating expenses truly are, you'll be able to build them into your monthly business budget and forecast them as accurately as possible.

Categorizing Your Operating Expenses

Once you've determined exactly what your operating expenses are, it's a good idea to group them into categories. You are likely to have several different types of expenses as you grow your side hustle, and by categorizing them appropriately, you'll be able to see very quickly which categories are driving your highest and also your lowest costs. It also makes it easier to build out your business budget when you have specific categories designated. For example, things like Facebook ads would fall under the expense category of advertising or marketing. If you hire someone to do paid graphic design work for you, that expense could fall under branding. For each of your categories, you can add a detailed description of what each expense was for.

As you categorize your expenses, you can use your own categories, but make sure you or your accountant can easily map them to the IRS business categories for tax purposes.

According to quickbooks.com and based on IRS guidance, some common business expense categories include:[1]

- Advertising and marketing
- Bank charges and fees
- Car and truck
- Commissions and fees, e.g., sales or referral commissions
- Contractors
- Dues and subscriptions
- Home office expenses
- Insurance
- Interest paid
- Licenses and fees
- Legal fees and professional services
- Meals and entertainment
- Office expenses
- Payroll expenses
- Rent and lease
- Repairs and maintenance
- Shipping and delivery
- Supplies
- Taxes and licenses
- Travel expenses
- Utilities
- Other business expenses that don't fit into any of the mentioned expense categories

Your operating expenses and your expense categories are things you'll need to identify early on in order to properly plan out your business finances. Mapping them out now helps you know what to expect and plan for later.

---

[1]https://quickbooks.intuit.com/learn-support/en-us/business-assets/
quickbooks-self-employed-schedule-c-categories-breakdown/00/369505

If you are a new business owner, you can do a review of your business plan and take some time to talk to some tenured business owners in your field to find out the types of expenses they have on a monthly basis. Alternatively, you can do some Google research to get a few ideas.

If you are a tenured business owner, I'd suggest going over a few months of business bank statements or reviewing whatever business accounting files you have. These will give you an idea of your historic operating expenses so you can decide what to keep or cut from your budget going forward.

Your operating expenses should also be reviewed on a monthly basis as part of your business budget review process (which we'll get into in the next section). These are expenses that can easily get out of control, especially as your business grows. If you don't keep an eye on them, expenses can quickly creep up and start eating into your business income and profits.

You can use a simple spreadsheet or simplified accounting software like FreshBooks, WaveApps, Xero, QuickBooks Online, etc., to track your expenses and keep them organized in categories when you are starting out. As your business grows, it's a good idea to consult with a bookkeeper or accountant to make sure you are on the right track.

Take Action

Depending on where you are with your business, now is a great time to plan out and estimate your startup and/or operating expenses so you know what to expect.

- Start identifying your anticipated startup costs and operating expenses based on what you've learned in this section.
- You can research existing businesses in your space and talk to other business owners to get a sense of other potential operating expenses that you may not have thought of so you can plan ahead.
- Once you have an initial list, you can organize them into categories for easy tracking. You can build a simple spreadsheet

or use a simplified accounting tool like FreshBooks, Xero, WaveApps, or QuickBooks to lay out your expenses and keep them organized. As your business grows, it's a good idea to consult a bookkeeper or accountant.

■ Once you get through this exercise, you'll have a pretty solid baseline estimation of the different expenses for your business.

YOUR BUSINESS BUDGET: AN ESSENTIAL PART OF YOUR BUSINESS SUCCESS

The same way you have a budget for your personal finances, you need to have a budget for your business finances. When you create a budget, you are essentially telling your money what to do on a daily, weekly, and monthly basis to grow your business and allow you to achieve your financial goals.

Your business budget is basically your money plan for your business, so having one is essential to managing your business finances successfully. Your budget will guide the expenditures you make in your business and help you stay on top of your business spending. I can't stress how important this is!

When you want to buy groceries, you'd create a list and reference the amount you have allocated to spend in your budget before you head out to the grocery store, right? (If your answer is *"umm,"* "I don't know," or "Don't talk to me," now is a great time for you to pick up my first book, *Clever Girl Finance, Ditch Debt, Save Money and Build Real Wealth*!)

You are probably very familiar with the fact that if you don't create a grocery list and you don't reference your budget, you can easily get distracted by all kinds of "amazing" food items at the store, load up your cart with more than you need, and return home as the not-so-proud owner of the entire aisle 16. Listen, you are not alone; I can totally relate because I've been there and done that. . .and yes, I've got the T-shirt (again) to prove it!

When you reference your budget, you are more likely to stick to your grocery list and you may even have money left over to put toward other categories in your budget like saving or investing!

Well, the same thing applies to your business. If you wanted to create a new product, you'd make a list of all the things you need to create it and reference your budget to determine how much you can (or cannot) allocate to this project to get started. On the other hand, if you don't have a plan and just "spend as you go," you are likely to run out of money, eat into profits, or put your business into an unnecessary financial bind. Over time, this lack of budgeting can put you out of business and deep into debt. Thus, having a business budget is super-important because you can properly allocate your financial resources, stay focused on achieving profitability as quickly as possible, build up a buffer of savings, and invest in growing your business over time.

Keep in mind, having a business budget is not always the same as using an accounting tool or software. While some accounting tools offer business budgeting features, most just track your actual spending and expenses. Your budget, on the other hand, allows you to plan ahead so you can see the full picture before you spend.

However, before we talk about how to create a business budget, I first have to discuss the importance of ensuring that your business finances are kept separate from your personal finances.

Keeping Your Business and Personal Finances Separate

Although you can use your personal money to fund your business initially, you need to ensure that you have separate bank accounts for your personal life and for your business and that you are keeping your financial transactions completely separate.

For one thing, keeping your finances separate will help you clearly understand how your business is really performing.

In addition (and very importantly), keeping your finances separate will help you avoid any issues with the IRS, which has strict rules around business financials and how they are tracked for tax purposes. Separate financials will also prevent you from violating any operating terms based on the type of legal entity you have, e.g., an LLC or a corporation.

Co-mingling your finances can be confusing, cause you to pay more taxes than necessary, and even get you in trouble with the IRS (high penalties and back-calculated interest)—and you definitely don't want any problems with Uncle Sam!

If you are using personal funds to start your business, here are four key tips:

1. **Adjust your personal budget to account for the funds you'll be putting into your business.** This way, you won't impact your other expenses and personal finance goals and you can plan accordingly. If you are using a credit card, make sure the credit card is designated only for business expenses.

   Caution: When leveraging debt to start a business, it's essential that you have created a strategy of how you'll be paying this debt back.

2. **You can designate the personal funds you deposit into your business as an equity investment in your business or as a loan from you to your business that your business has to repay back to you in the future.** Be sure to keep track of the dates and the specific amounts.

3. **Deposit the designated personal funds into your business account.** From there, make all your business transactions using your business account, not your personal account.

4. **When your business starts to make money, you have a couple of options.** You can either reinvest the earnings back into your business so your business can become

self-sustaining or create a plan to pay yourself back the loan you made to your business.

To open your business accounts, you'll need your Employer Identification Number (EIN), the official paperwork for your registered business, and one or more forms of personal identification (depending on what the specific bank requires). If you are unsure, you should consult with an accountant to help you set up these structures.

With that being said, let's get back to budgeting. There are two key steps to creating a solid business budget: forecasting your income and forecasting your expenses. Let's go over each one.

Forecasting Your Business Income

As part of your budgeting process, you want to be able to forecast your potential business income, as well as track your actual income so you know how much your business can potentially earn versus how much it is actually earning. While you may not be able to perfectly predict your business income, here are a few steps you can take:

Compare your business to other existing businesses. If you can, talk to owners of tenured businesses to find out what their sales were like when they were at your stage as well as what they did to drive those sales.

Determine what types of activities could drive sales for you. For instance, is there a certain type of advertising you can do? Can you restructure your services or repackage your products in a certain way?

Base your forecast on volume. How many products will you need to sell to make X amount of money?

Again, there's no exact science to forecasting your business income and it's not meant to be 100 percent accurate. The goal of forecasting your income is to get you thinking, planning, and researching how much money you could make. Don't be afraid to create different scenarios. The most important thing to keep in mind with forecasting is that you want to set reasonable expectations for what your business can realistically earn over a period of time, given what you know and the specific action steps you can take to drive those earnings.

Forecasting Your Business Expenses

Similar to forecasting your income, you can also forecast your expenses. This step is a lot more straightforward than forecasting income, since you can't see the future and know how many sales you'll make, but you can easily research what things cost. When you create the expenses section of your business budget, you'll need to pull in the list of startup and/or operating expenses you created earlier. Once you've done this, the next thing you want to do is assign amounts to them (if you haven't already) and think through any potential reasons why your expenses could increase for a given month.

Your fixed expenses will not change much, unless you expect to add any brand-new fixed expenses. However, your variable expenses can be forecasted based on what expenses you think will increase based on your business growth or due to seasonality. For instance, if you expect a potential to sell 10 percent more products in a month (e.g., in a month with a holiday sale weekend) and you accept PayPal payments, then you can expect to have 10 percent more in additional PayPal commission expenses as well. On the other hand, if you expect a slow month, your variable expenses might be lower, but you should plan to have enough savings to cover your fixed expenses (since these won't typically decrease).

Again, these exercises are just designed to get you thinking and researching. For instance, if you're starting a wedding photography business, you can look up peak wedding months vs. slower seasons to help forecast your income and expenses.

Putting Your Business Budget Together

Now it's time to create your business budget. This is exciting—you are creating a plan that can make all the difference when it comes to the financial success of your business! (I know *budget* and *exciting* aren't often used in the same sentence, but stick with me!)

Creating your business budget doesn't have to be complicated, especially if you are just getting started. You can put it together in a simple spreadsheet with basic formulas. When laying out your budget, you want to include your expected or forecasted monthly business income as well as your monthly business expenses (including your startup costs if you are a new business owner and your recurring monthly operating expenses).

To make it easier, you can break things up into some categories, as discussed earlier, to keep things organized. Here's an example of columns to help you lay out a simple monthly business budget spreadsheet:

Month: _____

Income category	Income description	Expected amount	Actual amount	Difference (+ / −)
Product category 1		$	$	$
Product category 2		$	$	$
Service category 1		$	$	$
	Total	$	$	$

Expense category	Expense description	Budgeted amount	Actual amount	Difference (+ / −)
Expense category 1		$	$	$
Expense category 2		$	$	$
Expense category 3		$	$	$
	Total	$	$	$

Monthly Profit/loss (Actual income − Actual expenses)	$

This template, with preset formulas, is available via our free worksheet library at clevergirlfinance.com/worksheets.

As you lay out your business budget, keep in mind that this is a tool and reference that you are creating for the success of your business, so you want to make sure it makes sense to you.

You should plan to create your business budget in advance of each month. You can also create it for several months at a time and review things again ahead of each month. Once your budget is created, you want to make use of it by tracking your actual business spending against the budget you set, taking note of any variances or reasons why your budget came in over or under. This should be something you do often. It's a good idea to build a budget check-in into your weekly schedule.

Building Taxes into Your Budget

One important thing to keep in mind is that when your business starts to earn profits, you are likely to owe taxes to the government, so it's a good idea to build your potential tax obligation into your budget. A good rule of thumb, if you are unsure of your exact business tax obligation, is to set aside 25–30% of your business profits toward taxes in a designated business savings account. This way, you can cover your tax obligation without putting a strain on your business finances. If you have extra funds left over after tax season, you can reinvest the money back into your business or keep saving it for a rainy day.

It's also recommended that you make quarterly tax payments based on your estimated tax obligation. Per the IRS.gov website,[2] "Taxes must be paid as you earn or receive income during the year, either through withholding or estimated tax payments." It is also stated, "Individuals, including sole proprietors, partners, and S corporation shareholders, generally have to make estimated tax payments if they expect to owe tax of $1,000 or more when their return is filed."

An accountant can help you determine your specific tax rate and guide you as to how much you should be putting aside toward your tax obligation.

Take Action

Leverage the tips in this section to create your business budget and get ready to track your business income and expenses.

- You can build out your budget for several months at a time so you can plan, project, and forecast your business financials in advance. Be sure to review and adjust your budget as needed at least once a month, paying special attention to your expenses.
- Be aware of all your operating costs (i.e., how much you need to keep your business up and running each month).
- Plan for taxes. If your business is profitable, you will probably owe taxes, so build your estimated taxes into your business budget and save enough money to cover them. Be sure to talk to an accountant.
- Take advantage of an app or software to help you track your business's day-to-day finances. For example, FreshBooks, WaveApps, QuickBooks, etc.

---

[2]https://www.irs.gov/businesses/small-businesses-self-employed/estimated-taxes

■ If you'd like to use a business budget spreadsheet template, you can download ours for free as part of our business finances worksheet set available in our free worksheet library at clevergirlfinance.com/worksheets.

ANALYZING YOUR BUSINESS FINANCES: BREAKING EVEN, PROFIT, AND LOSS

Your business budget is the foundation of your finances, but there are other elements that are extremely important to track as well. Specifically, you need to understand how to determine your break-even point and calculate your business profit and loss. Let's start with how you can perform a break-even analysis for your products and services in a simple way.

Performing a Break-Even Analysis

Performing a break-even analysis helps you determine how much your business needs to sell to cover its total expenses (both fixed and variable) before it can become profitable. However, in order to successfully perform a break-even analysis, you need to know what your expected income is, as well as what your total expenses are. Once you know how much you need to sell in one month to break even (aka making enough to cover all your expenses, but not yet making a profit), you can set that as a business sales goal and start working toward it.

A simple formula you can use to perform a break-even analysis is as follows:

Your total fixed expenses

DIVIDED BY (÷)
The price of your products or services

MINUS (−)
The variable costs to produce each product or service

> **EQUALS (=)**
> *The number of products or services you need to sell to break even*

Let's go over this formula again with a realistic example. Let's say for the next 12 months, the total fixed expenses for your business come out to $5,000 and you have one product type that you will be selling for $20 per product. You've also determined that the variable cost to produce each product is $5, based on various factors, including the price of supplies for the specific time period. Based on these numbers and the formula we are using, the number of products you would need to sell in order to break even would be:

$$\$5,000 \div (\$20.00 - \$5.00) = \text{about } 333 \text{ products}$$

You can take the formula above and test it out for yourself, using your total fixed expenses, the price of your products or services, and the variable costs associated with producing your products and services.

Here's a simple spreadsheet where you can apply this break-even formula:

	Total fixed expenses	Price of product or service	Variable cost to produce product or service	# of products or services to sell to break even
Example:	$1,000	$50	$10	25
Product / Service 1				
Product / Service 2				
Product / Service 3				

This template, with the preset formula, is available for free via our free worksheet library at clevergirlfinance.com/worksheets.

Keep in mind that the variable costs associated with your products or services can change due to factors outside of your control—for instance, a change in the cost of supplies. You also want to keep in mind that the amount you use for your total fixed expenses should be based on the time frame in which you want to break even. For example, if you use your total fixed expenses for one month in this calculation, then the result you get will be the number of products you need to sell to break even in one month.

Tracking Profits and Loss

As a business owner, while breaking even is great, you ultimately want to earn profits—and a lot of them. So, let's talk a bit more about profits, and their flipside: navigating losses. In the early stages of your business, it's likely that your monthly business expenses may exceed your monthly business income for a while. This is normal, but it makes tracking your income against your expenses very important, because it allows you to see how close to (or far away from) earning a profit you are each month.

Regardless of what stage you've reached in your business, you want to track both your income and your expenses in your business budget so you can ensure you are keeping your expenses within your budget and aren't consistently operating in the red each month. Every dollar you spend in your business eats into your profits (or adds debt if you aren't yet profitable). And when you aren't tracking your spending, it's easy for money to disappear fast.

As business owners, we are sometimes guilty of disguising our overspending as "needs" for the business. From paid tools that you think will make your life easier, to fancy office accessories and furniture so your photos look cute for the 'gram, to upgrading features on your products and services that your customers may barely even notice, money can easily slip away and eliminate profits if you are not careful.

Keeping track of your profits versus your expenses can help you gain valuable insights about which specific areas in your business are driving the biggest profits or losses. These insights in turn can help you determine if you are overspending in certain areas that have minimal returns and if there is an opportunity to cut back in those areas. They can also help you determine which specific products or services are earning you more money than others. You can use this knowledge to focus on further promoting your best sellers as well as finding ways to improve, revise, or discontinue the products or services that aren't performing that well.

You can leverage your business budget to analyze your profits and loss by setting your budget up in a way where it also tracks the actual sales of your individual products and services. Here is the budget template I shared in the previous section that does just that:

Month: _____

Income category	Income description	Expected amount	Actual amount	Difference (+ / −)
Product category 1		$	$	$
Product category 2		$	$	$
Service category 1		$	$	$
	Total	$	$	$

Expense category	Expense description	Budgeted amount	Actual amount	Difference (+ / −)
Expense category 1		$	$	$
Expense category 2		$	$	$
Expense category 3		$	$	$

Expense category	Expense description	Budgeted amount	Actual amount	Difference (+ / −)
	Total	$	$	$

Monthly Profit/loss (Actual income − Actual expenses)	$

This template, with preset formulas, is available via our free worksheet library at clevergirlfinance.com/worksheets.

To analyze your profits and losses, you would focus specifically on the "actual amounts" for both your income (broken out by specific product and service) and your expenses. Your actual income minus your actual expenses will show you your overall profit or loss for a given month. Then, you can narrow in on each product and service category to determine which ones drove the profits or losses. A good accounting software can also help you create a profit-and-loss report based on your business transactions.

Take Action

Work on creating your own break-even analysis and assessing your profits and/or losses.

- ■ Using the suggestions in the section, work on performing your own break-even analysis to create a baseline of how much you'd need to sell each month in order to break even. Use the number you get to establish your initial sales goals.

- ■ As you run your business, set a reminder at the end of each month to review your budget and do a profit-and-loss assessment to gain additional insights for your business growth.

- ■ For spreadsheet templates to calculate your break-even point and to track your profits and losses, be sure to check out our business finances worksheet set, which is available via our free worksheet library at clevergirlfinance. com/worksheets.

PRICING YOUR PRODUCTS AND SERVICES

One of the biggest challenges business owners face is charging appropriately for their products and services. I personally struggled with this in the early stages of my various side hustles. When it came to pricing my products and services, I worried whether I was charging too much, so I ended up giving excessive discounts or not charging at all (especially with friends and family). As I scaled my businesses, I felt guilty about increasing my prices. Sometimes I was even put in awkward positions of having to say no to people who attempted to haggle my pricing even after I had clearly stated what my prices were. *Ugh. . .*the worst.

The problem with charging too low is that people may not associate the right value with your products and services. Essentially, cheap pricing may cause them to think your products are also cheap or not of good quality. If you have an amazing product or service, this perception could cause you to lose out on potential sales.

On the flipside, setting your pricing too high could also cause you to lose out on potential sales because your ideal customer is just not willing to pay that much. This can happen for a combination of reasons, like the perceived value of your products and services (just like with charging too low), who you are targeting, and what your competition is charging.

My friends Nike Olagbegi and Fisola Adepetu run a luxury children's party and social events planning company called the Art of Finesse, where they are known for their modern and detail-focused events. They shared their experiences with me on how they initially went about determining their pricing structure and how they were confidently able to charge more as their business grew:

> When we initially started, we actually were undercharg-ing. We noticed we weren't earning much profit for the work we were putting out. We had to sit down and do an analysis of market trends in our respective areas and from there we were able to adjust our pricing accordingly and ensure it was profitable for us. The amount of work and effort we put into each event made us feel comfortable charging more because we add value to each event and provide one-of-a-kind experiences. No one will believe in you if you don't believe in yourself. You have to believe your ideal client is out there and not everyone will be a perfect fit for you. You also have to be confident in your products and services in order to charge your worth. No one else can put a value on your time.

I personally had to learn how to determine the right pricing strategies for my business and how to say no when people were trying to take advantage of a personal relationship they had with me to get a discount or a freebie. While it was difficult to figure things out initially, this process only served me for the better when it came to growing my business and my profits.

If you are nodding your head because you can relate to all of this in one way or another, let's talk through how to price your products and services with strategies that actually work.

When it comes to pricing, there are a number of different strategies you can test and choose from. This way, you are not just assigning prices blindly with the hopes that maybe, just maybe, someone will buy from you.

By leveraging a proven pricing strategy, you can assign the best prices to your products and services, get paid what you are worth, and maximize your profits while still remaining attrac-tive to your ideal customers and staying competitive in your space. So, let's get into some common, yet effective pricing strategies!

- **Cost pricing strategy.** This strategy is ideal for product-based businesses. You'll start by calculating what it costs you to create each product. Once you've determined the cost per product, you can then add a markup to the price to include the total amount of profit you'd like to earn on each product. For example, let's say you sell scented candles, each candle costs you $12 to create, and you'd like to earn a minimum profit of $5 per candle. Your sales price would be $17 per candle.

- **Competitive pricing strategy.** With this strategy, your pricing is based on how your competitors are pricing similar products or services. By pricing your products and services slightly lower than your competitors, you can gain a competitive edge. This strategy can be beneficial if your products or services are in a highly saturated business industry.

- **Discount pricing strategy.** This is strategy is all about selling a product or service at a specific price normally but lowering the pricing during specific periods of time. For instance, you can offer discounts during a particular time of year (e.g., summer), during popular sales seasons (e.g., Black Friday), or when a product or service is being discontinued.

- **Premium pricing strategy.** This pricing strategy focuses on high-value brands with high perceived brand value. If you have established a solid and compelling brand identity, your perceived brand value can make up the difference for higher pricing.

- **What your customer is willing to pay.** With this pricing strategy, you intentionally sell your products and services based on what your ideal customer is willing to pay, which you can determine by researching and collecting data. One simple way to collect this data is to run surveys where your ideal customers can answer questions or select preset ranges of how much they might pay for specific a product or service.

- **Bundle pricing strategy.** Bundling products and services can be an effective pricing strategy because with a bundle you can compel a customer to buy more at a lower per-product cost than if they were to buy the products individually.

- **Freemium pricing strategy.** This pricing strategy is based on the idea that if you offer a free but valuable product or service add-on, you can compel your customer to pay for or upgrade to a full-priced product or service. For instance, "buy one get one free," "buy and get a free gift," and "try for free and upgrade for more" are all ways to leverage this freemium approach.

- **Psychology-based pricing.** This pricing approach is something that works on all of us subconsciously without our even realizing it. It could be the perceived lower value of a product or service because it's priced with a .99 or a .95 at the end. Or it could be a placement approach, where a lower-cost product or service is featured next to a higher-cost product or service, with the intent to get the customer to purchase the lower-cost offering. Psychological approaches to pricing also include the freemium and bundled pricing strategies as we discussed earlier.

Regardless of whichever pricing strategy you choose, I highly recommend that you always factor in what it costs to create the product or service. I also highly recommend testing out different pricing strategies and variations of the same pricing strategy to determine what works best for you.

Saying No

When it comes to friends and family asking for discounts or freebies, it's okay to say no and to stand firm on your pricing.

While there's nothing wrong with the occasional family and friends discount or freebie if it works in your budget, there are people who might expect this from you all the time! If it's easier for you, you can practice a specific response, or draft a specific email where you say no in a nice yet professional way. At the end of the day, you are in business to make money and you are spending your time and resources to make this happen. It's okay to say no to any situations that devalue your efforts or that do not serve the purpose of your business.

Appropriately pricing your products and services can be a challenge at first. But by testing, practicing, and keeping an eye on your numbers, over time you'll get to a place where you feel confident about charging your worth and increasing your prices accordingly!

Take Action

Now it's your turn to lay out your pricing strategy:

- Start out by selecting one or two pricing strategies that are relevant to your business and make a plan to begin testing them.
- Gather and assess your results after each test and implement the approach that works best for you.
- If you are struggling to say no to friends and family asking for discounts and freebies all the time, write down a response and practice saying it out loud. You can also draft an email and save it for when you need it.

MONEY MISTAKES TO AVOID WHILE BUILDING WEALTH WITH YOUR SIDE HUSTLE

When it comes to side hustles, money mistakes are all too common, and I'll be the first to tell you I've made tons of money mistakes while starting and running various side hustles. From overspending on things that had zero impact on my bottom line to assuming how quickly I would turn a profit without looking at my numbers, to not factoring in certain expenses that had a direct impact on my profits—I've been there, done that, and as you can already guess. . .I got *yet another* hideous T-shirt. Yeah, you don't want to see my hideous T-shirt collection!

On the other side of your mistakes are the incredible opportunities your business provides that can enable you to build long-term and life-changing wealth for you and your family. If executed properly, your business (even if it starts as a side hustle) can increase your income exponentially. When you own a business, your revenue is not limited by you having to wait for a raise, a bonus, or a promotion at your 9-to-5 job. And so, in this section, we'll be getting into the common mistakes to avoid and key tips to help you build wealth with your business.

Expensive Mistakes to Avoid with Your Business

While some mistakes in business are inevitable (after all, we sometimes have to fail in order to grow), there are some common mistakes that you can definitely avoid once you are aware of them. All you need is a little smart decision-making and good planning. The best part of avoiding these mistakes is that you could potentially save a ton of money, and I'm talking thousands of dollars, down the line.

Mistake #1: Overestimating how quickly you'll earn a profit. A lot of business owners assume they'll launch their side hustle and within weeks they will have a profitable business. That is rarely the case. In fact, it takes time to build a stable and consistently profitable business, so you want to build this fact into any plans you have, especially when it comes to paying your bills. If you are currently supporting your business by working full- or part-time, it's a good idea not to quit your job right away. You also want to make sure that you are budgeting, tracking your expenses, and performing a monthly break-even analysis so you can estimate as best as possible how soon you can expect to start earning a profit.

Mistake #2: Mixing personal and business funds. As highlighted earlier and worth stating again, mixing your personal and business funds is a big no-no. For one thing, it can be a nightmare come tax time in terms of determining your business profits or losses and taking the right business deductions. Outside of the tax problem, it's just really bad practice because you have no way of knowing how much your business is actually making or losing, which means you have no idea how your business is doing financially. Also, if you were to ever apply for business funding, you would have to show your business financials over time. If your personal and business finances are combined, you would have no way to clearly show this.

Mistake #3: Not staying on top of your business bookkeeping. Bookkeeping can be time-consuming and sometimes it can even get annoying. Trust me, I get it. However, a lot of business owners lose tons of money by ignoring their bookkeeping. And the longer you delay working on your bookkeeping, the more time-consuming and annoying it can be to catch up later. But you can work on adjusting your mindset and instead think of it as a key step you are taking to stay intentional about your money! As a business owner, staying on top of your bookkeeping is extremely important, and doing it frequently makes it easier. It's like washing dishes right after you use them instead of letting them pile up in the sink and giving yourself a bigger job later. Putting a couple of hours on your calendar each month to review your expenses and to stay on top of your invoices can save you a lot of headaches. There are lots of tools that can help make the process easier (e.g., QuickBooks, FreshBooks, Wave-Apps, etc.). Or, you can create your own simple spreadsheet tracking system, which is easiest if you're just starting out and don't have a ton of business transactions yet.

Mistake #4: Not planning for taxes. I've also mentioned this previously in the book, but it's worth mentioning again. As a small business owner, having a plan for taxes is essential. If you own a profitable business, you need to plan to put funds aside to pay the taxes you will owe the government. If you are not yet profitable, then you might be eligible for certain deductions based on your business expenses. Either way, you want to make sure you are prepared for taxes. An accountant can help you plan for this.

Mistake #5: Not hiring a good accountant. Speaking of accountants, having a good one is really important in your small business. Their role can go far beyond helping file your taxes and prepare for tax season. A good accountant will also provide you with recommendations that can save your business money, keep you up-to-date with the latest tax laws, and more. As your business grows, they can help you handle payroll, prepare annual statements and other documentation to support getting financing, etc.

Mistake #6: Not hiring a good lawyer. A good lawyer that handles small business matters can be very helpful as well. Your lawyer can help you with ensuring your business is properly registered and structured the right way in your state and from a federal perspective (i.e., choosing between a sole proprietorship, LLC, corporation, etc.). They can help you review all of your contracts and legal documentation, e.g., partnerships, vendor, and client contracts or any trademarks you may want to create. And if you were to get into any disputes with vendors or clients, they can give you legal advice and represent you if need be. While you might not need a lawyer right away if you feel comfortable getting your business registered on your own, it's never a bad idea to have a good lawyer on your contacts list.

Both your accountant and lawyer will save you valuable time and give you the peace of mind to know that things have been done the right way.

Mistake #7: Not establishing a business emergency fund. Establishing an emergency fund for your business works the same way one would work for your personal finances. It's there to protect your business in the event of an emergency. Your business emergency fund should be able to cover your business expenses (e.g., paying for the services you need to stay running, paying production costs, etc.) and keep you running for at least three to six months without you having to incur costly debt. There are folks out there who would tell you to get a business loan or line of credit that you can leverage in the event of an emergency, but I am of the opinion that if you are currently running a profitable business, you should create your own cash holding for your business in the event of emergencies and grow it as the business grows. Business loans are not free money. They come at a cost and that cost is in the form of interest. The longer it takes to pay back the loan, the more interest piles up and adds one more unnecessary expense you have to pay.

Mistake #8: Not having business insurance. While this is sometimes the last thing on a new business owner's mind, having business insurance is essential. Imagine if your computer gets stolen, or your retail store gets vandalized. If you don't have insurance, you are solely responsible for the replacement expenses. It's worth making a phone call to a reputable insurance agent in your location to discuss the various types of insurance available for your business—you may be surprised that it often doesn't come at a huge cost.

Mistake #9: Getting into business debt without a payoff plan. A lot of times, business owners take on business debt—in the form of credit cards or business loans, either from family and friends or a bank—without a solid plan of how these funds will be used in their business or how they will pay back this debt. They get sidetracked and may start spending the funds on stuff that is "nice to have" because they don't really have a strategic plan for the money. It is essential that before you consider any business funding that involves acquiring debt, you carefully plan out how the funds will be allocated and make a plan to repay the debt as quickly as possible.

Now that we've gotten the mistakes to avoid out of the way, let's talk about building wealth with your side hustle.

Tips to Build Wealth with Your Business

Starting and building a business is hard work. You already know this. And if you are putting in all this work, you should be able to reap the rewards. You are working so hard to build your empire that the last thing you want is for your efforts to be in vain. Your business can be financially game-changing; when you are able to build wealth, you gain freedom and you give yourself options. Creating options for yourself enables you to truly live your life on your own terms. So, when it comes to building wealth for your business, here are some key tips to keep in mind:

Constantly monitor your expenses. Your business expenses play a major role in the overall financial well-being of your business. Unnecessary expenses are the equivalent of little leaks on a boat and if left unrepaired, they can sink your entire vessel. So, make a plan to frequently review your expenses and eliminate any that are no longer serving your business. Also, be sure to periodically look out for cheaper alternatives to save more money.

Create multiple streams of income within your business. While your business in itself is an investment and (hopefully) an asset to create another income source for you, you can make it even more valuable by diversifying your business income streams. This essentially means seeking out multiple opportunities for your business to generate revenue and profits. You could do it through creating additional product and service lines, investing some of your earnings in a business brokerage account (yes, you can do this!), or creating a spin-off business that caters to a different niche or target audience. When it comes to investing on behalf of your business, many of the larger brokerage firms like Fidelity, TD Ameritrade, and Charles Schwab offer this service.

Pay yourself based on business profitability and reinvest in your business. It can be tempting to cash out all the profits you make from your business to pay yourself a salary, especially as it first starts to earn money. But it's also important to remember that in order to sustain and grow your business to achieve your bigger goals, you are going to need to reinvest in your business. Consider paying yourself a smaller salary, based on how your business is doing, while leaving room to keep some of your profits in your business and dedicate those funds toward its growth. As your business grows, you'll then have the ability to pay yourself a larger salary and invest even more into your business, but you have to give your business the opportunity to achieve that growth first by not constantly cashing out all of your profits.

Establish a business emergency fund. I highlighted the lack of an emergency fund as a mistake earlier, but it's also key for building wealth with your business. An emergency fund should be part of your business game plan so that in the event of an unplanned situation—for instance, if business is slow or you need to hire fast to fulfill a production opportunity—you have the cash to get through the situation without having to leverage credit cards, take out loans, or give up business equity because you desperately need money.

▶ **NOTE**

Giving up equity can be a strategic move to help you scale your business and can be a win–win for all parties involved. However, you want to make sure you are carefully considering how much equity you give up and to whom and not be forced to do it because you are in financial distress.

You might need to work full- or part-time until your business becomes fully profitable, and that's okay. As you build your side hustle, especially in the early stages, you'll need a steady source of income to pay your bills and keep your household afloat, especially if you have dependents and other financial obligations. So, don't quit your day job just yet. If you find that you absolutely need to quit before your business is earning solid revenue, it's okay to get a part-time job to support your financial obligations while you make more time to focus on your business. There's no shame in working for someone else while you build your empire behind the scenes! While you continue working, you should definitely take advantage of any wealth-building opportunities your employer offers like Health Savings Accounts (HSAs) or retirement accounts like the 401k and 403b. Doing this will ensure you are still able to build long-term wealth even if your business is taking time to get on its feet.

Remember your business is an investment for your future self. Think of your business not just as a temporary income boost, but an investment in your future self where the potential payout can be massive. So, learn as much as you can, test, pivot, and do what's necessary to grow, knowing that all the hard work is a sacrifice now for a bigger payoff later.

Take Action

- Review this section to determine what actions you need to take now and in the near future to avoid the common business mistakes I covered.

- Next, create a list and a plan of action for the key steps you can take to start leveraging your business to build long-term wealth. For instance, designating a specific amount of money into a business savings account, opening up a business investment account, determining ways to generate multiple streams of income in your business, etc.

MEET SAHIRENYS PIERCE

Sahirenys is the founder of Poised Finance and Lifestyle (thepoisedlifestyle.com) and a Latina millennial mom of two. As a first-generation college graduate with a degree in finance, she knew her community needed help in the area of personal finance because financial literacy isn't something that has been socially normalized or taught. So, instead of making financial literacy feel overwhelming or confusing, she created Poised to educate and empower women about money. In doing so, she's created systems like the High-5 Banking Method and the Standard Operating Procedure (SOP) to navigate financially difficult times. These tools help women build their financial confidence so they can manage their finances and lifestyle with poise.

How did you identify your startup expenses and set up your business budget when you first started your side hustle?
Since my husband initially started our journey into entrepreneurship, our creative agency already had everything I needed to start my own business and so my startup expenses were minimal. We picked my website layout, company name, and took a few headshots, and *boom*, my business was here. All of this was very cost-effective, so we were able to cash flow the expenses from our business savings. For me it was important to maximize the money we earned from our businesses to cover our mandatory needs. Knowing how much our lifestyle, health care, and all the other business expenses cost allowed us to create our personal budget and our business budgets. Once we saw how much money would be required to meet our minimum requirements, we then set a goal to save $300 to $500 each month to reinvest in our businesses. Some months we would use the funds and other months it would just collect for future use. We didn't base

these savings on a percentage of our income because that could change from month to month. It was important for us to calculate a baseline of how much we wanted to save to realistically hit our financial goals for the businesses. Meaning that our savings baseline might be $300 a month to cover annual expenses, but we would save an additional $200 for any additional services we might need or things we wanted to do business-wise. We focused on saving with purpose, knowing that some of the money was for a specific need and the rest was to reinvest as needed.

You are a mom to two young kids running a side hustle and your husband runs your other business full-time. How did you plan your personal finances to support this?
Because I am a full-time mom to two toddlers, my goal was to keep my business as a side hustle until they got older. I am still on that journey as it takes time for kids to grow up and go to school. My husband, however, transitioned his own side hustle into a full-time business, but before this happened, we made sure we focused on our personal finances first. We wanted to make the transition as smooth as possible, so we lowered our expenses by paying off debt and built an emergency fund beforehand. Once we became entrepreneurs, we realized that this journey comes with a lot of risks and we needed to prioritize our family's well-being. So, we decided to pay our recurring bills in advance and push all income toward taking care of our financial obligations first. This meant paying up any bills for the year before saving for a new computer or accomplishing personal goals. We continue to leverage this approach today. Once our responsibilities are taken care of, whatever we make after is a bonus. Having our personal finances in order allows us to navigate the many ups and downs of entrepreneurship with financial peace of mind.

What's been most challenging for you when it comes to your business finances?
The most challenging thing about our business finances is deciding how much to pull out for our family's personal finances. If we

pull out all of our earned income, then we won't have enough money to invest back into our businesses. But it's important for us to have funds saved to reinvest in our businesses, whether it's to upgrade old equipment or to get new services. The best way we've been able to do this is to have separate business savings for short-term goals. This way we have the funds already available to pay for new services or equipment as we see fit. The truth is, as your business matures, you need to become more efficient at making money, and you have to work smart. So, finding services or people that will save you time is going to benefit your business.

What are you most proud of as it relates to your business finances?

I am proud that our businesses are completely debt-free and have been built on a strong financial foundation. Because my husband and I did the initial work to dramatically lower our cost of living, we reduced the requirement of how much our businesses need to make to take care of our personal finances. When I first started my own business, it was important for me to feel good about it. Since my business first started as a hobby, I didn't want to feel like it was hurting my family's finances. We positioned my business to make sure it was a positive benefit for me and our family by maximizing the rest of our income to cover our necessities, wants, and goals. This means my business income is not a necessity for our family to run smoothly and do everything we want to do. This move allows my business income to be more flexible when it comes to reinvesting in my business, myself, and our family's goals. I like this because if my business income slows down, it doesn't affect my personal finances. At this point, my business income is an asset. And if we hit hard times in our other business, I know that my business income is adding a plus to our family's finances. This in turn allows us to have a backup plan to generate income no matter if we're going through good times or bad times financially.

So many people overlook taxes, especially when it comes to their side hustle. How do you manage planning for your taxes?

We personally have a Certified Public Accountant (CPA) that we consult with. Every year we make sure to get an accurate estimate of our quarterly taxes, so we can budget appropriately. On top of that, we have a specific savings account where we save for our quarterly taxes. This was our first savings account for our businesses since we didn't want to underestimate taxes and get in trouble with the IRS. At the end of the year, if we overpaid, we put that money toward the following year's taxes. Any money that's left over in our tax savings account gets reassigned to our short-term business goals savings account.

What advice can you give someone trying to get a handle on managing their business finances?

Simplify your finances by having separate business bank accounts, create a realistic budget, and set goals to reinvest in your business. It is so important to be realistic with your business finances and not pull out every penny your business makes. If you do, this will limit your savings ability for your business and make it difficult to reinvest in your business. I recently read that Alphabet, the parent company of Google, spent $26 billion on research and development in 2019. If the largest companies in the world are investing in themselves, then why aren't we doing the same for our businesses? Of course, we're not going to spend billions like these tech giants. But it does go to show that if you want to stay in the game, you have to make reinvesting in your business a line item of importance.

CHAPTER 6

In It to Win It!

Know your metrics, stay consistent, and manage your time well.

LEVERAGING METRICS IN YOUR BUSINESS

One of my favorite parts of managing my business is assessing my metrics! Your business metrics are basically performance indicators that showcase how well your business is doing. This is extremely important because it can help you get a sense of what's working well (and what's not), what's driving sales, and what needs to be adjusted. All of these insights will help you make better business decisions and track your progress, and they can even help you identify problems before they get out of hand.

In my photography business, one of the first metrics I started tracking were the most popular blog post categories on my website. Thanks to this, I found that my rustic wedding photography category was the most-visited category on my website. This gave me insights as to what type of bride my work attracted. Using this knowledge, I focused on showcasing more of these types of pictures on my site, through social media, and in my portfolio albums, which in turn helped me attract more of these brides to generate more revenue.

With Clever Girl Finance, the metrics we track today are much more robust. We track things like page views to determine how many visitors come to our site and what specific content is resonating with our readers; social media engagement to see what our audience is talking about; social media content reach to determine how impactful a brand partnership has been; and month-over-month changes across various metrics categories to see how we are doing overall from a growth perspective.

You can leverage metrics to track pretty much any part of your business that you want to focus on, but there are some metrics that you may need to look at more closely than others. I would suggest tracking and assessing your metrics on a monthly basis.

Financial Metrics

Metrics relating to your business finances, some of which we touched on in the prior chapter on business finances, are really important to understand. Some key financial metrics you'll want to pay attention to each month include:

- **Fixed costs.** These are the costs you need to pay for regardless of how your business is doing and essentially represent your overhead. Tracking these helps you stay aware of any cost increases that happen and gives you a baseline for how much revenue you need to make at a minimum to cover these costs.

- **Variable costs.** Your variable costs are typically tied to the creation and production volume of your product and services. Tracking this metric helps you get a sense of if and how your revenue is changing when your variable costs change.

- **Total sales or revenue.** This metric is one that every business owner should absolutely be tracking so you are aware of how much money your business is making as a whole from your different products and services.

- **Average sales or revenue.** Knowing your average revenue is another metric that is good to track, because you'll be able to compare your average revenue to your monthly costs to see if your revenue is covering your costs on average each month. Sometimes those high months can be deceiving if you also experience low months, so it's a good idea to know and track your averages.

- **Sales goals.** Knowing what your sales goals are for each month, quarter, or year will help you stay on top of tracking your progress when it comes to all the activities required to make the needed sales.

- **Profit margin.** This metric helps you gain a clear picture of what your true profits are when you subtract your expenses from your revenue. The goal is to widen the gap as much as possible between the two, so your revenue exceeds your expenses by a large margin. Tracking this metric will keep you mindful of your expenses and can help you think creatively when it comes to your sales strategies.

Marketing Metrics

Being able to attract your ideal customer means you need to have a marketing strategy in place, and you need metrics to measure the effectiveness of your strategy. Some key marketing metrics that are a good idea to pay attention to include:

- **Customer acquisition rate.** This metric measures the rate at which you are acquiring potential customers from specific activities on your various acquisition channels. For instance, how many people signed up to your email list from reading an article on your website, or from visiting your website via your Instagram profile, or from clicking one of your product images on Pinterest? Knowing your acquisition metrics can help you decide on which channel to focus your time and efforts.

- **Conversion rates.** This metric is defined as the number of conversions (sales, signups, or other desired actions) divided by the total number of visitors. For instance, you can track the number of sales you make based on the number of visitors to your product or services pages via your different customer acquisition channels. Or you could track the number of your Instagram followers who visited your Instagram shop and made a purchase. You can even use conversion rates to track how effective your Facebook ads are based on the number of sales they return. Knowing your conversion rates can help you fine-tune your marketing strategy.

▶ **NOTE**

What is a good conversion rate? Depending on your specific industry or niche, a good sales conversion rate can be anywhere from 2 percent to 10 percent. It's worth doing some research for your specific space to get a better sense of what number to use as a baseline.

- ▪ **New vs. returning customers.** Another good metric to track is your new vs. returning customers. Who is visiting your product or service pages and making purchases? Are you getting a lot of repeat customers? Knowing this metric can help you determine if there is an opportunity to retarget either of these customer categories with ads to incentivize them to make additional purchases.
- ▪ **Social media engagement.** While this metric does not necessarily translate to sales, it's worth tracking to get a sense of what your customers are talking about and the questions they are asking. This engagement can also give you a sense of brand loyalty. Social media engagement metrics include things like comments, likes, and shares. The insights you gain can be used to improve your marketing strategy and even your products and services. Take note of anything customers are saying about things they wish your product or service had.

Tools to Track Your Business Metrics

Now that we've gone over a baseline list of potential metrics you can track, you are probably wondering exactly how to track each of them. One great way to keep it all in one place is to create a simple spreadsheet that has a list of the metrics you want to track each month.

You can pull metrics from your business budget and from the various analytics and insights features available today on each of the social media platforms. For example, you can leverage the "insights" section of your account on Instagram and the "analytics" section on Pinterest to pull specific metrics you want to track each month.

Another incredibly powerful and free tool that you can use to track how customers are using your website is Google Analytics. This powerful tool can help you analyze your website traffic, which is incredibly important because your website is your home base. You can track the actions visitors take on your website (pages visited, landing pages, exit pages, time spent), gain insights about the demographics of your visitors (age, location, interests, etc.), and even set sales and revenue goals tied to specific products or services on your Google Analytics account. I highly recommend using Google Analytics—it's totally worth the time it takes to set it up for your business website. Google offers a great tutorial for beginners on using Google Analytics, which you can find at https://analytics.google.com/analytics/academy.

As I've mentioned, tracking your metrics can help you gain some really good insights to help you increase your sales and grow your business. However, there are a ton of metrics you could potentially track, and you don't want this process to become overwhelming or stressful. Decide on the metrics that are core to achieving your business goals and start there.

Take Action

Now that you know the importance of tracking your business metrics, get started with yours.

■ **Create a list of metrics most relevant to your business goals to begin tracking.** Keep in mind that you don't need to track every single metric available, just the ones that are most relevant or impactful to your business right now. You can always add on others later.

- **Organize the metrics you want to track in a spreadsheet by month over the next 12 months.** To make it easier, you can set this up as a separate tab, or "sheet," next to your business budget spreadsheet if you are using Microsoft Excel or Google Sheets.
- **Set up your Google Analytics accounts for your website.** If you are unsure how to do this, check out the free tutorials Google offers at https://analytics.google.com/analytics/academy.
- **Dedicate time each month to review the metrics you are tracking.** Pay close attention to any trends you see and make a note of any key actions you took throughout each month that affected your metrics. Use this information to brainstorm ideas to grow your future revenue.

MANAGING YOUR TIME: TIPS AND TOOLS TO HELP

As a business owner, time is one of your most valuable assets, especially if you are starting your business as a side hustle on top of your full-time job and other obligations (kids, family, life!). Since you're a busy woman, you want to make sure that you are spending your time on the right types of activities—activities that will make you money.

Unfortunately, many business owners end up spending way too much time figuring out administrative tasks or getting distracted from the core of their business by the next pretty, shiny object so that they eventually find themselves feeling overwhelmed. Their business becomes a burden and is no longer the exciting project they were eager to work on every day. However, that's not going to be you, because in this section, we are going to walk through how you can create a plan to help better manage the limited time you have. We'll also go over the types of tools you can leverage to help you minimize the stress.

Your time management has a direct impact on your business finances. The more effectively you can get your administrative and other tasks done, especially the recurring ones, the more time you can spend doing the things you love in your business and, of course, making money!

Creating a Schedule

The first thing you need to do to effectively manage your time is to identify all the different aspects of your business that you need to work on in order to make money and grow. Once you have this list, you can then research and plan the steps required to execute each aspect, assign time on your schedule for each step, leverage tools to automate certain areas, and determine what areas you'll need to delegate or hire for over time.

Some examples of the different tasks and responsibilities in your business include:

- **Administrative tasks.** Business metrics, research, emails, website management, product and service development, etc.
- **Financial tasks.** Budgeting, expense tracking, taxes, invoicing and payments, other bookkeeping, etc.
- **Sales and marketing.** Email marketing, blog posts, videos, podcasts, social media content, running webinars or workshops, etc.
- **Customer service and management.** Communications, purchase and returns management, product shipments, service delivery, gathering feedback and testimonials, etc.
- **Partnerships and collaborations.** Onboarding affiliates, brand partnerships, joint promotions, etc.

The steps you assign on your schedule could be daily (social media posting), weekly (newsletters, blog posts), monthly (metrics, budgeting), quarterly (specific sales campaigns), and perhaps even annually (reviewing annual subscriptions and services). The whole idea is to identify the task you need to work on and assign a specific time to get it done so you can focus on other areas of your business and life.

Tools to Help You Save Time and Money

Certain types of tools can be incredibly helpful to ensuring you are managing your business in the most effective way. These tools will save you time and potentially help earn you lots of money.

I'm going to share some of my favorites here (at the time of this writing) but be sure to do your own research, ask other business owners, and find what works best for you, as there are constant improvements with existing tools and new tools are always being released.

- **Calendar management and scheduling.** acuityscheduling.com, calendly.com, youcanbook.me
- **Online payment collection.** paypal.com, stripe.com, square.com
- **Online accounting & invoicing.** quickbooks.com, waveapps.com, freshbooks.com
- **Payroll management.** gusto.com, quickbooks.com
- **Project and task management.** asana.com, basecamp.com, trello.com
- **Overall business management.** 17hats.com, zoho.com, kalohq.com
- **Email reminders.** boomeranggmail.com
- **Email list management and communications.** convertkit.com, mailchimp.com, mailerlite.com
- **Social media management.** hootsuite.com, later.com, buffer.com, tailwind.com
- **Virtual receptionists.** callruby.com
- **Freelancers (e.g., virtual assistants, web developers, graphic design).** fiverr.com, 99designs.com, upwork.com, freelancer.com

Tips for Making the Most of Your Time

As you lay out your tasks, make a schedule, and begin to experiment with tools to make your life easier, here are six key tips to help you make the most of your time:

1. Plan ahead by creating a schedule for your day, week, and month.
2. Prioritize your tasks in order of importance or urgency.
3. Delegate tasks as often as you can.
4. Leverage tools to help you automate tasks.
5. Assess how each day and week went, noting areas you'd like to change or improve.
6. Eliminate distractions while you work, for instance, by muting social media and alerts.

Take Action

Effectively manage your time by identifying and prioritizing the various tasks that need to be done in your business.

- Write down a list of all the different kinds of responsibilities in your business, as well as the required steps you need to complete for each task. A simple spreadsheet is a great place to manage this.
- Build the various steps into your schedule based on how often they occur (e.g., daily, weekly, monthly, quarterly, or annually).
- Make a note of areas you need to delegate or would like to hire for.

WHO DO YOU NEED ON YOUR TEAM?

When I first started Clever Girl Finance as a side hustle, I was a team of me, myself, and yours truly. I was working full-time, mothering my twin toddlers, and trying to grow my side hustle. As a team of one, it meant that I did it all. Not only was I the CEO and sole decision maker, I was also the content creator, the receptionist, the assistant, the social media manager, and the intern. Add that onto my full-time corporate job and the jobs I did for my family as a driver, cook, cleaning and laundry lady, teacher, and more—I had a lot going on.

Needless to say, I was in a perpetual cycle of exhaustion. I wasn't in a position to pay anyone from a business that was not yet making money, and I was trying to figure out how to make my side hustle work. But despite it all, it was an incredibly exciting time for me. I was doing something different than what I did every day at my corporate job, and it was something that was very meaningful to me. I was also enjoying the process of working through all the different ideas I had, and I was learning so much.

There were many sleepless nights and sometimes I felt overwhelmed, but the experience of starting out solo and figuring out how to make it work was worthwhile. I gained valuable experience working through all the different aspects of my business, learning what I didn't know, figuring out how to make things work, and identifying the areas where I would eventually need help.

As you are reading this, you might be in a similar position—you have so much going on in your life and on top of it all, you are trying to start or run a side hustle on your own. The value in starting out this way, however, is that you get the opportunity to work through all the aspects of your business. Even if you aren't an expert in certain areas, you'll figure out enough to get by in the interim, then hire and train someone to support you when the time comes. Because if you stick with it and are able to get your business on its feet, there *will* come a time when you'll be able to start hiring people and assembling your team.

Getting Ready to Expand Your Team

With Clever Girl Finance, it took me two and a half years to get to the point where I was able to make my first permanent hire.

Prior to that two-and-a-half-year mark, I was able to hire contractors for the one-off jobs I needed to be done, and I made it work that way. This is an option you can leverage as well.

As you start to think about where you need help and how to find the right resources, here are some things to keep in mind based on my experiences and lessons learned.

- **Identify where you need support.** Based on the different aspects of your business you laid out in the previous section and the specific steps required to complete each category and task, identify where you need help the most and prioritize that need. Do you need a designer, a social media manager, an assistant, a writer, a developer? This exercise will help you get clear on where you have the most pressing need.

- **Create a job requirement.** Based on this, create a job requirement of the skill set the ideal candidate would need to have in order to support you successfully in this role.

- **Take your time to hire.** Ever heard the saying *hire slow but fire fast*? Well, it rings true. When you take your time to hire by going through an interview process with potential candidates, taking time to determine if they are a good fit for your brand, checking their references, and speaking with them at least a couple of times, you are less likely to have hiring regrets. It's definitely true that sometimes even if you've done your due diligence, things don't work out, but by taking your time to make your decision, you can minimize your chances of a bad hire.

- **Have hiring contracts in place.** It's also really important to have a contractual agreement in place for anyone you hire so the terms of their employment are clear. This contract should clearly highlight any trial periods (I'd highly recommend at least a 30-trial period), payment terms, working hours, and the job description.

■ **Hire on a contract basis until you can hire part-time or full-time.** As I mentioned, prior to my being able to hire a permanent position for Clever Girl Finance, I needed help in certain areas, so I hired on a per-job/contract basis. It worked well for me based on my business budget at the time. Even if you can only hire on an as-needed basis, it can make a huge difference in getting tasks done, especially if you are working on a tight timeline.

■ **Set the right expectations.** Once you've hired who you need, it's important to set the right expectations from the beginning of their working relationship with you, even if you've only hired on a per-job basis. Take the time to train and communicate with them often. And be sure to provide them with feedback as time progresses, giving them time to learn your workflow and improve their work if necessary. Keep in mind that there is a chance that things might not work out. In this scenario, it's important that you let the person know and cut your losses as soon as possible.

The Value of Business Peers and Mentors

As a business owner, having a support system is incredibly important. While your friends and family can try to support you along the way, what they can offer tends to be more "moral support" than practical guidance. Having business peers going through the same entrepreneurial journey and mentors who have business experience can be extremely helpful, especially when you are trying to figure things out, navigating a difficult period in business, or experiencing amazing growth and need some support or guidance. They can also be the ones to encourage and give you the push you need to take the next big step in your business that might be outside of your comfort zone.

In my personal experience, I've found that building a business can be very isolating and lonely. And having a peer to talk through a situation and to encourage and motivate you can make a huge difference. While your business peers might be at different stages of their journey, the one thing you have in common is that you are traveling a similar path, and that alone can make the whole experience less lonely. Your peers can share their experiences, provide suggestions, and even be the test subjects for your products and services!

Having experienced mentors (or in a formal role, advisors), on the other hand, can provide you with specific advice and guidance based on their own business experiences, including their successes and failures. Depending on their industry experience and connections, they can also be great motivators and can help with making key business introductions. You can also have multiple mentors that support you in different areas of your business. For instance, you can have a mentor who has deep marketing experience and another who has experience with product development.

How Do You Find Business Peers and Mentors?

Finding business peers and mentors is all about relationship building: meeting people and spending time getting to know them. One way to start is within your personal network. Once you get intentional about seeking out peers and mentors, you may be surprised about who you are already connected to within your network.

For instance, some of your friends, acquaintances, or former colleagues may have business ideas or might have even started businesses they have not shared broadly. One of my amazing mentors is actually a former boss of mine who just happens to be a serial entrepreneur with an in-depth knowledge of business strategy and development. But funnily enough, I had no idea about his experience. It wasn't until a couple of years after I left that particular job and was talking to a former coworker about starting a business that they suggested I get reconnected with this particular mentor, and I'm so grateful they made that suggestion.

Another way to seek out peers and mentors is through introductions from people you are connected to. I can't tell you how many new entrepreneur friends I've made from other people introducing me to people within their network, many of whom I am still constantly in touch with.

You can also make time to participate in entrepreneur-focused events (online and in-person), participate in entrepreneur communities and groups, and even engage with other entrepreneurs on social media. Thanks to the internet and the evolution of social interactions online, it's become so much easier to meet other people. However, it's going to require that you are intentional, and you might need to step out of your comfort zone, especially if you are somewhat introverted like me.

Sometimes it's a challenge for me to meet people, but I make the effort. It helps to do things like add reminders to my calendars or send the introduction request email or text message before I can talk myself out of it!

Finally, you might decide to hire a coach to guide you through certain aspects of building your business. If you choose to go this route, be sure to do your research to make sure they can truly help you, have the experience, and very importantly, that they are a good fit for your personality and style.

Take Action

Let's work on identifying who you need on your team and finding business peers and mentors!

- ◾ **If you are looking to hire someone to support your business, review the specific aspects of your business and identify the key tasks where you need assistance.** Use this information to create a job description that clearly defines the role, even if you are only hiring on a per-job basis to start with. You can put the word out through your personal network, your business audience/ community, by asking for referrals from people you know, or by making a job post on an online freelance platform like fiverr.com, upwork.com, etc. Be sure to take your time when it comes to vetting each potential candidate.

- **If you are looking for business peers or mentors, create another description that highlights specifically how you'd like a mentor to support you.** Start with your personal network and ask for introductions from people you are connected to already. You should also seek out and join entrepreneur communities (they could be within your niche and industry) and build relationships that way.

MEET EMILIE ARIES

Emilie Aries is an author, CEO, and founder, speaker, and podcast host. After rising quickly in the world of campaigns and elections as a grassroots organizer and digital strategist, she launched the award-winning personal and professional development company Bossed Up (www.bossedup.com) in 2013.

Today, Emilie and the Bossed Up team provide research-driven, impact-oriented training programs both online and in-person to serve their ambitious community of women who crave the tools and tactics to assertively advocate for the careers and lives they want. She is based in Denver, Colorado, and combines her political past and personal experience with burnout to help others step into their power and be the boss of their careers and lives.

You lead a busy life running multiple businesses. What time management and money-saving tools and processes have you implemented to maximize the time you have available to run the various aspects of your businesses?
I live and die by my Google calendar, which my entire team has access to. I use it to block out time for recurring tasks I know I

need to make a priority each week, including my own financial reflections and projections, management tasks like biweekly reviews for all my staff, and creative tasks like writing, podcasting, and recording social media content. I also believe in the power of batching work: for example, I try my best to consolidate client coaching calls and program trainings on Tuesdays, Wednesdays, and Thursdays, while reserving Mondays and Fridays for more administrative, management, and big-picture strategy work. By reducing my switching costs, I find I'm able to be more focused and productive on those public-facing days while making space to be more creative and free-wheeling on "backstage" days with my team.

I also use Calendly, which cuts down on wasted time emailing back and forth to schedule calls. It shares my availability (with boundaries on my time that I set) with my clients and partners who can schedule one-on-one calls with me. It's been a huge time-saver and really made those long email chains trying to find the best time for both of us a thing of the past.

When it comes to big-picture planning and goal-setting, I struggled to find a good system out there. So, after years of studying the science of sustaining motivation, I collaborated with cognitive scientists and academic researchers who study gender and role overload to develop my own planner and goal-tracking system specifically designed to help ambitious women mitigate guilt. We started testing our method, which I call the LifeTracker Planner, back in 2013 at every single Bossed Up Bootcamp. After years of testing and refining it, today we now have a worldwide community of women who thrive as they strive alongside me each and every year using our planner.

One of the best strategies inherent to this method is highlighting: the temporary prioritization of one area of your life over another. This means first setting goals across work, love, wellness, and other areas of life (which can be anything but often includes personal finance, travel, or artistic goals) and then highlighting—or choosing—just one area of life to make your priority that month. I can't tell you how liberating it is to be able to proactively say, "I'm not making my health and wellness goals my top priority this month. My financial goals take precedence." The reality is: all our goals are important. But rarely are any of them truly urgent. By highlighting, you're creating a self-imposed sense of urgency that only lasts one month. So, it kind of forces you to make those trade-offs ahead of time so you don't feel guilty when life happens and you have to make tough choices about where to spend your limited time and energy anyway.

What kinds of metrics do you leverage in your business, and how do metrics play a part in your business earnings and growth?
We set financial projections that serve as our primary benchmarks: total number of unique clients and gross revenue. All other KPIs (key performance indicators) are related to lead generation: unique website visits, consultation calls scheduled, email list subscribers, podcast downloads (listens), and followers on social media. Those are indicators of new prospective clients, but what we're mostly focused on is converting our passive browsers into buyers. That requires continued creative energy put toward increasing our conversion rates on our landing pages and communication channels. We're constantly experimenting with new marketing channels and website landing page improvements to try and increase our conversion rates and new client acquisition. At the start of the pandemic in early 2020, most of our creative energy was put toward new product development as we converted our entire business model to something scalable in a remote environment. But once we developed new products and services, we refocused our attention on marketing and client acquisition.

You have remained consistent year after year in business. What has helped you get through difficult times?
I have remained resilient, sure, but I wouldn't say consistent. My business has taken many forms over the past seven years, constantly evolving and changing along the way. They say

necessity is the mother of all innovation, and that's been true for me. I bootstrapped my business and have never taken on any investment or loans (until the PPP SBA loan program in 2020). So, I've had to remain agile in order to keep my lights on and continue to operate at a profit. Looking back, I had no idea what I was doing when I started, but I was committed to learning and evolving along the way. I remained open to trial and error as a teacher, and have learned so much through putting in serious sweat equity and countless hours. Now, seven years in, I feel much more confident in my business prowess. Once you learn the fundamentals of starting, growing, and running one business, you can start any business. You can learn those fundamentals in theory in school, sure, but you can also learn them through trial and error. My educational background in political science and cognitive science taught me a lot about people, human motivation, systems, and persuasion, all of which have served me well. But I learned business one real-world win or loss at a time. Some of those mistakes along the way have been very costly, but nothing insurmountable. The reason I've stuck with this business, in particular, is because I've pursued the kind of work that feels inevitable to me, it feels like an extension of who I am. Bossed Up feels so fully and entirely aligned with how I want to show up in this world, I don't think I'd do anything else, even if I won the lottery tomorrow. I followed my passion, and I've worked hard to find a way to make it yield my own paycheck. I created the community I needed myself.

What advice would you give someone starting a side hustle about thinking long-term, time management, and perseverance?
If you're going to start your own business, you might as well go for the business you really want to start. Don't just pursue a side hustle for the money. You have to be in it because you're obsessed with the industry or subject matter or your vision.

The money matters, of course, but it's secondary. The money won't keep you going when things are tough: your belief in your vision and your ability to make a meaningful impact will. Be willing to put in the time, energy, and effort up-front. Once you've proven your concept, then focus on how to make things more scalable, manageable, and sustainable. Starting is hard—but it's just the first step.

CHAPTER 7

Plan for Growth

Pursuing growth means thinking long-term.

STAYING CONSISTENT AND PERSEVERING THROUGH SEASONS

Building a business is not easy. In fact, at times it can be incredibly difficult. Your dreams are so big, but you have no idea how you will possibly attain them and the road just seems so long. As business owners we go through all kinds of emotions. There are ups and there are downs, there are highs and there are lows. But I'm going to tell you this: trust the process. Staying focused and consistent and picking yourself back up when you fall are incredibly important on this journey.

I've yet to meet a business owner who said the journey has been completely smooth sailing. As a matter of fact, it's usually the opposite. But despite how challenging building a business can be, there is value in persevering through all the various seasons, keeping your goals front and center, and not giving up.

In the first year of starting Clever Girl Finance, I made $200. Yup, you read that right, $200. This after coming off a side hustle that had made me almost $70,000 in one year. I was seeing people start businesses and within a few months they were making six figures and quitting their jobs. What the heck was I doing telling women to be clever about their finances?!

But instead of giving up (even though I wanted to a thousand times), I stayed firm in my belief of my vision and in my mission to help women succeed. And so, I continued to put in the work and learn as much as I could, many times by trial and error. I leaned on my business peers and my mentors for the support I needed and I kept going. I tested some ideas that were complete flops (and a waste of my hard-earned money) but by taking the lessons and applying them, I was also able to pivot and develop ideas that were big successes. Slowly, but surely, I started to make progress, generate revenue, build a team, and ultimately quit my job. Today, I run my business full-time and I have no regrets about the process or the journey. Looking back at my journey, however, here's some advice I'd like to share:

- **It's okay to continue to work full-time until you get your side hustle on its feet.** With every single one of my side hustles, I always had a full-time job. With Clever Girl Finance, I worked full-time for two years before I transitioned into my business full-time. While social media makes it seem glamorous to quit your job immediately to run your business, there's nothing glamorous about not being able to pay your bills. While I was working, I focused on saving money to cover my financial obligations before I quit my job. Doing this also gave my business the opportunity to get on its feet without the financial strain of not having a consistent paycheck. It's perfectly fine to work full-time while you build your business and figure things out. Your business revenue doesn't have to entirely replace your income before you quit your job, but you want to make sure that you are still able to pay your bills. There's also absolutely nothing wrong with keeping your side hustle as a side hustle!

- **If needed, work part-time to pay your bills while you dedicate more hours to your side hustle.** I mentioned this earlier in the book, but it's worth repeating. You may find that you get to a crossroads where your business is doing well and you need to dedicate more time to it in order for it to grow. If you aren't quite at your revenue goals or you need to keep some specific benefits that you are not yet ready to bear the full cost of (e.g., health insurance), getting a part-time job may be a good idea. There's no shame in doing what you need to do to pay your bills.

- **Review your business plan often and adjust it accordingly.** Your business plan is an ever-evolving document that can help you stay focused and keep track of changes in your business. If for whatever reason things are not working out in your business as expected, revisit your business plan to restrategize and pivot as needed. Sometimes minor or even major pivots from your original idea are necessary, especially as you learn more about running your business, your audience, and developing your products and services.

- **Address your blocks head-on and commit to moving forward.** Sometimes one of the biggest challenges we face with getting a business up and running or taking the next big step is ourselves getting in our own way. Self-doubt, fear, and all kinds of other blocks always find a way to surface throughout your journey. These blocks stall your progress or, even worse, make you give up. However, when you start experiencing these blocks, as opposed to letting them become all-consuming, it's important that you face them head-on. List out your blocks, and alongside each one, create an action that you can take to counter the block holding you back. Very importantly, remind yourself why you started.

- **Acknowledge and celebrate your wins.** As business owners, we sometimes get so focused on the next thing we need to do that we forget to pause and acknowledge the progress we've made. But acknowledging and celebrating your wins is very important! It can serve as the motivation you need to stay focused and keep going and also help you counter some of the blocks you may experience.

- **Don't compare yourself to others.** Comparison is the thief of all joy. It can be completely demoralizing to see someone else's business take off after only a short period of time when you've been toiling away for so long. However, it's important to remember that everyone's journey is different and sometimes you don't truly know what someone else's experience has been if you are on the outside looking in. Your journey is uniquely your own, and all good things will happen with time.

■ **Lean on your support system.** Finally, I highly recommend that you lean on your support system, because that's what they are there for—to support you. Trust me, you'll get to a point where you need help from your family, friends, business peers, and mentors. There's no shame in asking for help—plus, at some point you will likely be in the position to help someone else who needs support as well.

Take Action

If you need to, bookmark this section to revisit it when you need that extra motivation to keep going. You can also create your own list of advice to follow and keep it easily accessible so you can review it often.

PRIORITIZING SELF-CARE

There's no way I can write this book without talking about the importance of prioritizing your self-care, especially as an entrepreneur. Remember all those jobs I told you I had? Sometimes doing too much can be detrimental. All the things I had going on as a wife, mom, business owner, and at the time, full-time corporate woman, makes me sound like Superwoman, but that couldn't be further from the truth.

A couple of years into running Clever Girl Finance, I woke up one day and could barely get out of bed. The entire room was spinning. Every time I would try to get up or move my head, it felt like I was riding a rollercoaster. I couldn't even make it to the bathroom because I couldn't stand up on my own. My kids' school day was canceled because I couldn't get out of bed and I couldn't drive them to school. Work was canceled. Meetings were canceled. After-school activities canceled. Even making dinner was canceled. My mom and my mother-in-law ended up having to come around to help me, and my world stayed spinning for three whole days. During this time, outside of going to see the doctor, all I could do was lie in bed and close my eyes. I couldn't watch TV, I couldn't read a book, I couldn't do anything.

I had developed vertigo. Specifically, migraine-induced vertigo that came about as a result of the severe migraines I would often get, which were triggered by stress, barely sleeping, and basically doing too much, compounded over several months. Let me tell you, having migraine-induced vertigo is no fun. I ended up on all kinds of migraine medication, I had to undergo therapy for three weeks to combat vertigo, and I couldn't drive for a couple of months because my depth of field was off.

That experience was the reality check I needed to prioritize my self-care. It showed me that if I didn't take care of myself, then eventually, I wouldn't be able to function at all in any aspect of my life. Today, prioritizing self-care means setting fixed working hours. It means taking the help family offers or getting a babysitter when I need extra help. It means leaving my laptop at home when I go on vacation and leaning on my team to support the business while I take a break. It means making time to work out, go for a walk, binge-watch a TV series, read a good book, or just be quiet and sit still. Now when I'm overdoing things (which if I'm being really honest, still happens sometimes), and I'm on the edge of a migraine, I know it is absolutely time to stop. Like, drop everything and STOP.

As a business owner with a busy life, I totally understand that there's always so much to do and there are not enough hours in the day to get it all done. We live in a culture where if you are not showing how hard you are hustling, then you are not doing enough. But it's important to keep in mind that building a business is a marathon, not a sprint, and you need to be well in order to build. Yes, the idea of the perpetual hustle seems cool, but it's not sustainable long term if you don't give yourself a break every now and then. So, as you make plans to build and grow your business, be sure to include time for your self-care and mental wellness in those plans as well.

Take Action

Prioritizing your self-care is incredibly important. Plan to make time for yourself frequently and give yourself the breaks that you very much need.

- Be intentional about prioritizing your self-care by blocking off time on your schedule, even if it's just for a few minutes each day, where you are not working or worrying about other people.
- Take a day or weekend off often where you can disconnect and recharge.
- Determine other ways in which you can prioritize self-care.

MEET EBONY RUFFIN

Ebony is the founder and managing member of Ruffin Consulting Services (www.ruffinconsultingservices.com), a business consulting firm providing life insurance solutions to families and business owners. Through her business, Ebony has made life insurance an attractive topic to discuss. As a result, instead of clients running away from life insurance, thinking of it as a death benefit, they are attracted to life insurance as a financial tool and wealth benefit. The key to her business success is her focus on education first. Specifically, she teaches her clients why life insurance is an integral component to a financial plan. Her goal is for the world to know Ruffin Consulting Services as the company that changed the narrative of life insurance from a death topic to a wealth topic.

You started your business as a side hustle and continue to run it as such. What were some mistakes you made starting your side hustle and how did you overcome them?
Ruffin Consulting Services has successfully operated while I continue to offer my expertise in accounting and finance in

corporate America. The core of Ruffin Consulting Services, which is life insurance education, was birthed through my experience in childhood, college, and corporate America. Through my experience, I have created a formula that allows me to thrive in purpose by offering my expertise in finance and accounting to corporate America and life insurance education to my target market.When I initially started my business, my back-end operations were very manual and I was not leveraging social media. I allowed my personal decision not to have personal social media pages carry over into my business decision not to have business social media pages. These distinct areas presented an opportunity to refine my business model to operate more efficiently. I started by leveraging automation to make my business processes less manual, but in a way that wouldn't compromise the customer's experience and still be inclusive of my integrity, character, and personality. When it came to social media, I quickly learned that I had to think differently with my business. People want to go directly to your Instagram and Facebook page to get a bird's-eye view of you and your business. A website and business card are simply not enough. I also had to overcome appearing so "corporate" on social media and appear more "social"—I mean, that's why it's called social media, right! I hired the right help and I was coached through the process of not hiding behind Instagram templates and perfect corporate captions and instead, allowing my personality to show. The progress is evident if one decides to review the Instagram page from its inception to now. With consistency, I found my business voice and target market. The response was overwhelmingly positive. Business opportunities began to find me and ensured that I showed up as the same brand and voice on social media.

What type of people have been essential on your team in terms of helping your business grow?
The success of my business is directly correlated to having the right people in the right place to transition the business from "good to great," as quoted by my favorite author, Jim Collins.

Because I have an accounting background, I knew the importance of registering my business with the state, opening a business account, and establishing all the other various accounts and services in the business name. I hired a mentor to guide me with the launch of Ruffin Consulting Services on social media, specifically around what message to convey, establishing a tone, being consistent, creating calls to action, being relatable, and converting a comment or like to a business opportunity. The next key person I hired was a website designer. I was particular about finding the right person who would teach me the back end of my website so that I could be empowered to understand how it worked. As a result, I can manage the back end of my website with confidence. Next, I hired an automation specialist who assigned me the most important task of my business. She instructed me to write down my entire business process, which included marketing and prospecting, appointment scheduling, and helping a client through the end-to-end process of getting life insurance. This process was then transitioned from paper to automated systems for appointment scheduling and email management, which allowed me to have more time to focus on the big picture of Ruffin Consulting Services and be less consumed with the mundane processes. This answer would not be complete without mentioning my clients. My clients typically become repeat clients and have helped me establish a great referral system through positive word of mouth. I also have a Certified Public Accountant (CPA) who is instrumental to the financial stability of Ruffin Consulting Services. And last but not least are other business owners and entrepreneurs I have connected with. Ruffin Consulting Services has been featured on many platforms, and it's all due to building quality and trusting relationships.

How have you stayed focused on your entrepreneurial journey navigating the highs and lows of business?
I have remained focused by reminding myself that it's not about me, it's about my assignment in life. I understand my purpose in

Ruffin Consulting Services and because I am operating based on a purpose and not self, I am constantly encouraged. Quite honestly, I love life insurance, so it's easy for me to stay on the journey. Now, there are times where I have felt extremely overwhelmed by what I have to do, but implementing automation changed the game. Also, I have established business boundaries. My behavior communicates to everyone how to approach and perceive my business. Business boundaries help reduce, not totally eliminate, draining people, or "opportunities." It is also important to manage your time well. Life can have you in a whirlwind doing so many things, but time management and delegation will ensure that you do not burn out on the journey and quit. In summary, I stay focused because my business runs through my veins and it's my lifeline. It gives me divine purpose and I love life insurance.

Based on your experience, what pieces of advice would you give women who are building their side-hustle businesses?

Stay focused and stay in your lane. Be intentional and consistent. Be loyal to your business and establish boundaries with friends and family. It's okay not to be everywhere and always available; you have to focus. Automation, automation, automation; what are you doing manually that an automated process can simplify for you? Do your research and pay for the right services that will change your business. The best money I paid was hiring a consultant to implement automation in my business. Run your business like a business and not a hobby. Consistency is the best teacher and experience. By being consistent, you will learn what should be improved, what's working well, what your market is responding to, and so forth. Sometimes people want to ask a lot of questions about how you are getting it done, but if you just do the work, the answers will be evident.

In Closing

The road is long, but the journey is exciting, and you are more than capable of achieving your wildest dreams!

High-five girl, you've made it here! Now that you have gotten this far, I hope that you feel confident and excited about the incredible opportunity you have to build and grow a side hustle that can help you achieve your long-term life goals. That being said, here's a recap of some key things to remember as you go on your journey!

Key Takeaways to Remember

- **Get clear on your business vision and mission.** These are two really important pieces of building a successful business and they should align with your values and what's meaningful to you as an individual. Ultimately, you want to build a business you love!

- **Create a business plan that makes sense to you.** Remember, your business plan does not need to be a hundred- or thousand-page document. It can simply be a few pages that map out the details of your business in a way that makes sense to you. Be sure to revisit it often and don't be afraid to adapt it when you need to restrategize or pivot.

- **Get to know your ideal customer.** Getting to know your ideal customer is the equivalent of developing a relationship. Doing this will help you get clear on your product and service offerings, and it is foundational to building a successful business.

- **Create a brand your customers will love.** With so many businesses competing for the attention of your potential customers, your brand can be your key differentiator when it comes to your competition. Spend time establishing a look and feel for your brand that carries through your online presence, your storefront, and the actual products and services you have to offer.

- **Stay on top of your business finances.** Staying on top of your business finances is not just about how much money you are making. It's about understanding your expenses (both fixed and variable), monitoring and diversifying your revenue streams, and maximizing your profits. Not having a handle on your business finances is the quickest path to big problems, and you don't want (or need) that!

- **Watch your metrics to gain insights.** Your business metrics will essentially tell you how well your business is doing. By watching and analyzing them, you'll be able to see what's working well, what's driving sales, and what needs to be adjusted, so you can avoid issues ahead of time because you have the insight.

- **Be mindful of your time and prioritize your self-care.** You most likely lead a busy life, so planning, scheduling, and delegating are vital tools for helping you achieve a sense of balance and minimize stress. Don't forget to take time off to rest and recharge. There will always be work to do, but you come first.

- **Think long-term.** Patience is a virtue, and when it comes to business, it is also a necessity. While things might not happen as quickly as you'd like or exactly how you imagine them, don't lose sight of your big dreams and goals. Think long-term, take intentional action toward building your business, and don't give up—because your success is on the other side of every challenge in front of you.

Now it's on to building your empire! I'm rooting for you!

Index